making
a
living
in
CONSERVATION

making
a
living
in
CONSERVATION

a guide to outdoor careers

Albert M. Day

STACKPOLE BOOKS

MAKING A LIVING IN CONSERVATION
—A Guide to Outdoor Careers

Copyright © 1971 by
THE STACKPOLE COMPANY

Published by
STACKPOLE BOOKS
Cameron and Kelker Streets
Harrisburg, Pa. 17105

In the interests of conservation,

this book is printed on 100% recycled paper.

Price: $3.95

ISBN 0-8117-0964-7
Library of Congress Catalog Card Number 70-162449
Printed in U.S.A.

Contents

Acknowledgments

One of the satisfying aspects of writing a book of this nature is to acknowledge the assistance of others who spent their time and energies to make it possible; also to thank those who shared published articles and permitted quotes. To all, our sincere thanks.

We are particularly indebted to the following for their selection and provision of copies of position descriptions:

Mr. Richard A. Rosenberry, Executive Director, Pennsylvania Civil Service Commission.

Mr. William B. Barnes, Director, Indiana Division of Nature Preserves.

Mr. Robert W. Schoning, Oregon State Fisheries Director.

Mr. Robert W. Burwell, Regional Director, Bureau of Sport Fisheries and Wildlife.

Mr. Everett Doman, Director, Division of Wildlife Management, U.S. Forest Service.

Dr. J. L. Kask, formerly Assistant Director, U.S. Fish and Wildlife Service.

Miss Louise Gilmore, Asst. Personnel Director, National Park Service, and to Robert H. Weber, Director of Publications, Council of State Governments for reference material from *The Book Of The States*.

Conservation Occupations were taken in part from *Occupational Outlook Handbook*, issued by the U. S. Department of Labor. Sections dealing with Wildlife Conservationists, Fishery Scientists and Park Rangers are based on other official government documents.

I am particularly indebted to my wife, Eva Kendall Day, who continuously assisted in gathering material, typing and editing the manuscript, and provided counsel and aid.

A.M.D.

Introduction

Jobs in the out-of-doors hold a special appeal to many. They are becoming more important each year, as emphasis has shifted to problems of the natural environment.

Hunting and fishing were the chief recreational pursuits employing out-of-doors workers until the mid-Thirties. Then came new programs dealing with soil conservation, range management, forestry, wildlife management and pollution abatement.

As this trend continued, conservation, "the protection from loss and waste," gradually led to more emphasis on ecology, "the relationship of living organisms to their environment," and more recently, to concern for the environment or—"all the conditions, circumstances and influences surrounding the development of an organism." The most important "organism" is Man—you and me, our friends and families—our total civic body.

Action at all levels of governement, Federal, state and local, has been accelerated to meet the new demand. Even a reorganization of the Federal structure to pull together agencies and programs dealing with natural resources seems now more likely than ever before. States are forming environmental departments, private citizens are organizing groups which challenge programs that seem to jeopardize the natural environment. The Seventies promise to be the "Environmental Decade."

As emphasis on the domestic scene shifts from moon exploration, supersonic airplanes, wars, and costly foreign aid to the environmental issue, so jobs and employment shift with it.

Demand for out-of-doors jobs has never looked so promising. With the strength and substance of the growing awareness of environmental problems, this trend will continue.

New workers will be needed. Those who are the better trained will find the most rewarding careers. Many jobs require college degrees. Others require no more than high school education. Young people having an interest and a bent in this direction now have the best opportunity ever presented to make a career in conservation and the out-of-doors.

Agencies and groups responsible for these national programs cover all of America. The principal ones are:

Forestry: Federal, 50 states, and a growing number of private corporations and groups.

Parks: Federal, 50 states, county, municipal and private.

Soils: Federal, 50 states, counties, soil conservation districts, and private groups.

Sports Fish and Wildlife: Federal and 50 states, some private land use groups.

Commercial Fisheries: Federal and coastal states.

Environmental Health: Federal and 23 states.

The major employers of natural resource specialists are the state conservation agencies. These are variously organized as Departments of Natural Resources, State Conservation Departments, or Commissions of Game, Fish, Parks and Forestry.

The Federal Government also is an important employer of natural resource managers and scientists. Within the Department of the Interior, this includes the Bureaus of Land Management, Outdoor Recreation, Indian Affairs, Sport Fisheries and Wildlife, Reclamation, and the National Park Service. The Department of Agriculture includes the Forest Service, Soil Conservation Service and Extension Service. The U. S. Army Corps of Engineers also employs resource specialists, as do the Department of Health, Education and Welfare and the Atomic Energy Commission. The Department of Commerce has been assigned enormous new responsibilities with the creation of the National Oceanic and Atmospheric Administration.

Public service in the natural resources field is rewarding. Careerists interested in the out-of-doors reap satisfaction from being engaged in activities for the good of humanity. Their tasks go beyond the everyday "make a living" necessities of life. Cleaner water, purer air, more places where nature's bounties may be enjoyed by the average citizen—these are personal dividends above the very necessary monthly pay check.

Professions where trained people will be needed in increasing numbers as programs are adequately funded to provide a better natural environment include:

Civil Engineers	General Biologists
Sanitary Engineers	Soil Scientists
Oceanographers	Chemists
Chemical Engineers	Hydrologists
Microbiologists	Limnologists

Mathematicians	Ranges
Bacteriologists	Fishery stations
Entomologists	Wardens
Geologists	Fish and Game Propagators
Aquatic and Marine Biologists	Conservation Administrator
Planners and Economists	Land Management Specialists
Foresters	Photographers and artists
Managers	Public Relations Specialist
Parks	Outdoor Recreation Specialists
Forests	Conservation Advisers
Wildlife Refuges	

Salaries are good. No one will ever "make a million" from this type of public service, but he will be able to make a good living and lead a satisfying and productive life.

Federal retirement programs are excellent. A 6 1/2 percent salary deduction, with interest, affords old-age security unmatched by most commercial concerns. Mandatory retirement is age 70, although an employee may retire earlier under several different plans.

Annual and sick leaves are generous, up to 26 days a year annual; sick leave at 13 days a year may be accumulated indefinitely.

States are usually less generous than the Federal Government as to vacation leave. They range from 10 to 15 days, plus a varying number of local holidays, for elections, etc. Sick leave accumulations in most states have no limits, while in others 60 to 120 days are specified, earned at the rate of 12 to 15 days per year of service.

This book has been prepared to describe briefly the *kinds* of jobs available, approximate salary scales, types of work performed in the various fields, general educational requirements, employing agencies, and related matters.

This presentation differs from similar publications since it covers a much broader field of employment. Most literature issued by professional societies, authors and government agencies begins with the assumption that college degrees are essential—that conservation is a highly professional science. While this is true for the top level scientists and administrators, it does not necessarily hold for the army of workers at lower levels who carry out the day-by-day operations that make the various programs effective.

The top staff symbolically represents the one-eighth of the iceberg that rears its glistening peak above the ocean surface. Others represent the submerged seven-eighths that keep the structure afloat and steady.

This book attempts to focus on the broad spectrum—professional, sub-professional, and blue collar workers at Federal, state and industry levels. All are important.

A casual perusal may leave the reader with the impression that the salary scales included are low. Please remember that these job descriptions cover workers with only high school education as well as those with Ph.D. degrees. Normally, the greater the education, the higher the pay. Few top jobs are described because these are attained after years of experience and training. Rather, the emphasis is on the lower grade, beginning jobs which afford the opportunity to start at the bottom and work up, in traditional American fashion.

These points should be kept in mind when considering the choice of a career.

[1]

The New Focus
on Conservation

Predictions are precarious. National goals and trends change with the shifting needs of people. Job opportunities change accordingly.

Not long ago, the demand for engineers, chemists and electronic experts practically assured that a person graduating from college in the field of science would find immediate employment in the aerospace or war-related industries. Scouts combed the campuses seeking bright young men and women during their undergraduate years with promises of a rosy future.

Now, national budget cutbacks have had their effect on many military and space-associated programs and opportunities in some of the science fields are fluctuating more widely than before. There is even said to be a disappointed and disillusioned surplus of young graduates in the engineering professions who are willing to consider other employment opportunities. Training programs, of course, are being organized to provide other jobs for such surplus categories somewhere in the "new movement" which, ironically, had a part in bringing about this change in national mood—concern for the environment.

EVERYONE WANTS A CLEAN ENVIRONMENT

Public awareness of the importance of a clean environment did not occur overnight. National parks, forests, wildlife refuges and the wilderness areas had their inception at the turn of the century. The depression days of the Thirties, charac-

13

terized by unemployment, drouth, dust bowls and public panic, spawned soil conservation and land reclamation reforms. The decade of the Sixties saw a steady growth of interest in pollution abatement and the curbing of industries that fouled the air and water with factory wastes.

Interest in conservation gradually spread from a handful of hunters and fishermen to the masses. Evidence increased that hepatitis, polio, and other human diseases could be traced to unsanitary water conditions; Rachel Carson's *Silent Spring* warned of the ultimate dangers from excessive uses of DDT and other insoluable pesticides; political figures at all levels of government gradually realized that this business of cleaner water and air made good sense to more than just trout fishermen, pleasure boaters and water skiers. Creating a better environment has become everybody's business.

The decade of the Sixties saw great progress. There came into being a National Recreation Policy, expansion of existing conservation programs, the Bureau of Outdoor Recreation, Federal grants-in-aid for more out-of-doors programs, the Multiple Use and Classification Act to improve administration of Public Domain —one-third of the nation's land—a Water Quality Act, Clean Water Restoration Act, Wilderness Act, Endangered Species Act, and many others of a similar nature.

Of greatest significance, the public began to realize that this nation cannot forever foul its own nest without certain retribution. The importance of protecting the environment in which we all live assumed national concern.

CONSERVATION JOB OUTLOOK

The adjustment in national priorities has materially influenced the conservation job situation. Between 1960 and 1969, in the Department of the Interior, where more conservation bureaus are located than in any other Federal department, the Park Service showed a percentage increase in employment of 46.9; Sport Fisheries and Wildlife 55.7; Commercial Fisheries 47.3; and Land Management 47.7. In contrast, the Bureau of Reclamation recorded 0.2, Water and Power 10.9; and Geological Survey 21.9 percentages.

States followed the same pattern, due in part to Federal grants-in-aid for national programs. Some even exceeded the Federal pace-setting trend.

The decade of the Seventies promises to outstrip the accomplishments of the Sixties. During 1970, Congress found itself swamped with some 4,000 environmental-related bills to consider. Many were enacted, including those to improve water and air quality and recover solid wastes. Action was taken to create a World Environmental Institute and an Environmental Education Act to support programs in environmental education from pre-school to adult levels.

Only a short time ago, Congress took under consideration a group of the most far-reaching ecology, anti-pollution-oriented proposals ever to be considered in American history. Main concerns center about preventing and reducing air and water pollution on the one hand and environmentally improving use of the nation's land on the other.

Proposals included are: increased funds for the construction of municipal waste treatment facilities; an Environmental Financing Authority to underwrite local bond issues; banning the dumping of wastes in the oceans, coastal waters, and the Great Lakes; land-use legislation to better control mining operations and location of power plants; bringing parks closer to centers of population; authority to set noise standards; limiting the use of pesticides through permits; and other nationally-oriented and supervised controls to halt and reverse the trend toward further deterioration of the environment—everybody's environment. The encouraging aspect of this change in national priorities is the fact that it is now bi-partisan.

MORE TRAINED PEOPLE ARE NEEDED

A famous crusader in the environmental field three decades ago often said: "The worst enemies of conservation are Republicans and Democrats." That was "Ding" Darling, noted Iowa cartoonist whose pungent drawings of the rape of our natural resources became classics. His messages are as pertinent today as they were then. If he were alive today and could see the unanimity of thinking in high places among political figures in both parties, he would probably say: "Gad! It simply can't be true."

The vastly increased interest that has lately surfaced above a complacent "business as usual" public attitude has created a situation unequalled in American history.

Strengthening old laws, enacting new ones, detecting dangers, building evidence to hail offenders before the courts of the land, publicity, discussions—all of the aspects of an aroused public movement, are bound to have effect.

Trained people are needed in increasing numbers to do the job. Talk, laws, even appropriations do little except to guide public and private agencies toward action. Action means people on the job—people who know what needs to be done, and more importantly, how to do it.

Many skills with various degrees of training are needed. The field is immense—practically as large as our complicated culture, because the problems affect all of us. For someone who is interested in a clean wholesome life in the out-of-doors doing things which are bound to benefit future generations, here are fields that should be seriously considered.

The pages that follow describe typical occupations and, in general, the details of what is expected in various jobs. Note the salary ranges, but keep also in mind that in many of the positions, those employed are often provided living accommodations. And there are a number of important "fringe" benefits. Some jobs are in areas relatively isolated, especially during the winter. Yet a great number of them offer a chance to live in the most scenic parts of a state—or even in all America!

[2]

Careers in Forestry

Forests are one of America's greatest natural resources. They cover more than one-third of the land area of the country. Foresters manage, develop, and protect these valuable lands and their resources—timber, water, wildlife, forage, and recreation areas. They estimate the amount and value of these resources. They plan and supervise the harvesting and cutting of trees, purchase and sale of trees and timber, the processing, utilization and marketing of forest products, and reforestation activities (renewing the forest cover by seeding or planting).

Foresters also safeguard forests from fire, destructive animals, insects and diseases. Other responsibilities of foresters include wildlife protection and watershed management, and the management of camps, parks, and grazing land.

Foresters usually specialize in one area of work, such as timber management, fire control, forest economics, outdoor recreation, watershed management, wildlife management, or range management. Some of these specialized activities are becoming recognized as distinct professions, the profession of range managers, for example.

Foresters also may engage in research activities, extension work (providing forestry information to farmers, logging companies, and the public), forest marketing, and college and university teaching.

PLACES OF EMPLOYMENT

An estimated 25,000 persons were employed as foresters in the United States in 1968. About one-third were employed in private industry, mainly by pulp and paper, lumber, logging, and milling companies. Slightly less than one-third were employed by the Federal Government, mainly in the Forest Service of the Department of Agriculture. Other Federal agencies employing significant numbers of foresters were the Departments of the Interior and Defense. Most of the remainder were employed by state and local governments, colleges and universities, and consulting firms. Others were managers of their own lands or were in business for themselves as consultants.

QUALIFICATIONS AND CAREER OPPORTUNITIES

A bachelor's degree with a major in forestry is the minimum educational requirement for young persons seeking professional careers in forestry. An advanced degree is generally required for teaching and research positions.

Education in forestry leading to a bachelor's or higher degree was offered in 1968 by 48 colleges and universities of which 32 are accredited by the Society of American Foresters. The curriculums in most of these schools include specialized forestry courses in five essential areas: (1) Silviculture (methods of growing and improving forest crops); (2) forest protection (primarily against fire, insects, and disease); (3) forest management (the application of business methods and technical forestry principles to the operation of a forest property); (4) forest economics (study of the factors affecting the supply of and the demand for forest products); and (5) forest utilization (the harvesting, processing, and marketing of the forest crop and other forest resources).

The curriculums also include related courses in the management of recreational lands, watershed management, and wildlife management, as well as courses in mathematics, science, engineering, economics, and the humanities. Most colleges require that students spend one summer in a field camp operated by the college. Forestry students also are encouraged to work other summers in jobs that will give them firsthand experience in forest or conservation work.

Beginning positions for forestry graduates often involve work in a broad range of relatively routine activities under the supervision of experienced foresters. As they gain experience, foresters may advance to increasingly responsible positions in management of forest lands or related research activities.

Qualifications for success in forestry include an enthusiasm for outdoor work and the ability to meet and deal effectively with people. Many jobs also require physical stamina and a willingness to work in remote areas.

EMPLOYMENT OUTLOOK

Employment opportunities for forestry graduates are expected to be favorable through the 1970's. Among the major factors underlying this anticipated demand are the country's growing population and rising living standards, which will tend to increase the demand for forest products and the use of forests for recreation areas. Forestry and related employment also may be favorably influenced by the growing awareness of the need to conserve and replenish our forest resources.

Private owners of timberland are expected to employ increasing numbers of foresters to realize the higher profitability of improved forestry and logging practices. The forest products industries also will require additional foresters to apply new techniques for utilizing the entire forest crop, to develop methods of growing superior stands of trees over a shorter period of time, and to do research in genetics and fertilization. In addition, competition from metal, plastics, and other materials is expected to stimulate further research to develop new and improved wood products.

The Federal Government is likely to offer increasing employment opportunities for foresters in the years ahead, mainly in the Forest Service of the Department of Agriculture. Among the factors expected to contribute to this expansion are the demands for the use of national forest resources, the trend toward more scientific management of these lands, and expanding research and conservation programs in areas such as outdoor recreation, watershed management, wildlife protection, and range management.

State government agencies also should offer additional employment opportunities for foresters. Forest fire control, protection against insects and diseases, provision of technical assistance to owners of private forest lands, and other Federal-State cooperative programs usually are channeled through state forestry organizations. Growing demands for recreation facilities in forest lands are likely to result in expansion of state parks and other recreational areas.

College teaching and research in areas such as forest genetics, forest disease and insect control, harvesting and reforestation methods, forest products utilization, and fire behavior and control are other avenues of favorable employment opportunity for foresters, but primarily for those having graduate degrees.

In addition to new positions created by the rising demand for foresters, a few hundred openings will arise each year due to retirements, deaths, and transfers out of the profession.

Opportunities for women in outdoor forestry is somewhat limited, largely because of the strenuous physical requirements of much of the work. The few women presently employed in forestry are engaged chiefly in research, administration, and educational work; future opportunities for women also are likely to be primarily in these fields.

Beginning salaries of foresters employed by state governments vary widely; but, with a few exceptions, they tend to be lower than Federal salaries. Entrance salaries in private industry, according to limited data, are fairly comparable to Federal salary levels.

Forestry aides, called forestry technicians at higher career levels, assist foresters in managing and caring for forest lands and their resources.

An estimated 13,000 persons were employed as forestry aides in 1968. About 5,000 were employed by the Federal Government; the Forest Service of the U. S. Department of Agriculture employed approximately 3,000 of these. Approximately 2,000 were working for state governments. About 6,000 were employed in private industry, primarily by lumber, logging, and paper milling companies. Forestry aides also work in tree nurseries and in forestation projects of mining, railroad, and oil companies.

Employment opportunities for forestry aides are expected to increase rapidly through the 1970's. Prospects will be especially good for those having post-high-school training in a forestry curriculum. As the employment of foresters continues to grow, increasing numbers of forestry aides will be needed to assist them. Also, it is expected that forestry aides will assume some of the more routine jobs now being done by foresters.

Private industry is expected to provide many additional employment opportunities for forestry aides. Forest products industries are becoming increasingly aware of the profitability of employing technical persons knowledgeable in the practical application of scientific forest practices.

A LOOK AT TYPICAL FORESTRY POSITIONS

Management of the nation's vast forest lands requires a wide range of specialization with various degrees of responsibility and professional competence. Foresters develop and manage areas for timber, water, soil, forage, wildlife, minerals, recreation and the land. Forestry technicians and aides of various specialties assist the Forester. Among the most important are those whose duties encompass forest and range fire control.

The Federal Government employs forestry workers throughout the United States and its possessions. All states have forestry departments. Timber industries employ many professional and nonprofessional workers in all sections of the country.

A few typical job descriptions follow.

Forest Trainee

A beginning assignment which introduces the employee to professional practices and provides him the opportunity to apply his schooling to situations in the forest. Foresters or Forest Technicians supervise the training process. This is usually a *seasonal* position.

Education: Completion of a freshman year in forestry from a recognized college or university.
Salary Range: $6,000– $7,500.

Forester 1

Personal professional development is obtained by performing productive tasks, which may include cruising timber, participating in fire suppresion activities, inspecting logging operations and providing forestry advice to private landowners.

Education and Experience: Bachelor's degree in forestry or related option.
Salary Range: $7,500–$9,600.

Forester 2

Assists in making studies and administering a forestry program or organizes, coordinates and supervises forestry activities in an administrative unit. Duties may include supervision of forest management and timber sales, livestock grazing, public recreation, fire control and conducting technical studies.

Education and Experience: College degree in forestry and one year technical forestry experience, or two years forest technology training and three years technical forestry experience.

Salary Range: $9,000—$11,000.

Forester 3

Staff assistant working in specialized technical forestry program involving fire control, range or timber management, recreation, wildlife, or as consultant to administrators. As field supervisor, may act as district forester of a moderate-sized district.

Education and Experience: Bachelor's degree in forestry and successful work performance comparable to Forester 2.

Salary Range: $10,500—$13,500.

Forester 4

Position may entail duties as a staff assistant or as a district forester, directing all activities within a unit of major size and importance.

Education and Experience: Bachelor's degree in forestry and successful performance of work at lower level.

Salary Range: $13,500—$17,500

Forester 5

A staff role as a program director, responsible for a major forestry program, or as an area director, responsible for all activities in several regions or districts.

Education and Experience: Bachelor's degree in forestry and demonstration of successful performance in progressively difficult administrative or research work in the fields of forestry.

Salary Range: $15,000—$19,000.

Forest Lookout

Responsible for detecting, locating and reporting forest fires from a lookout tower, particularly during periods of relatively high danger of forest fire occurrence.

Education and Experience: One year of experience in forest protection work and completion of at least an eighth-grade education.

Salary Range: $4,500—$6,000. *Seasonal.*

Forest Patrolman

Patrols an assigned area to detect and suppress forest fires, directing volunteer fire fighters as needed.

Education and Experience: At least an eighth-grade education plus one year of experience in forest fire work.

Salary Range: $4,500—$6,000. *Seasonal.*

Excerpts from an actual state civil service job description for such a position in an Eastern state are as follows:

• • •

An employee in this class travels through sparsely populated and heavily wooded areas during periods of high forest fire danger to prevent, detect, locate, report and assist in the suppression of forest fires. On fire suppression employee may direct a group of volunteer fire fighters or may work as member of a special fire crew. Assignments are received in the form of general and specific instructions and work is checked by a superior warden and by review of reports.

EXAMPLES OF WORK PERFORMED:

Patrols an assigned territory to prevent, detect, locate, suppress and report forest fires.

Acts independently or as a member of a group of stand-by fire fighters ready to report to a forest fire and initiate control measures in the least possible time.

Constructs and maintains forest roads, trails, telephone lines and other facilities during periods of low fire danger.

Acts as leader of temporary fire fighters on forest fire suppression.

Prepares daily reports of activities and submits to superiors for review.

Performs related work as required.

REQUIRED KNOWLEDGES, SKILLS AND ABILITIES:

Some knowledge of forest fire prevention and fire control methods and techniques.

Ability to perform unskilled and semi-skilled work in the maintenance of towers, buildings, telephone lines, roads, trails and fire fighting equipment.

Skill in the use of the common tools used in construction and maintenance work.

Ability to understand and follow oral and written instructions without close supervision.

Ability to supervise a small crew of forest fire fighters.

Good physical condition.

• • •

Nursery Foreman

Skilled supervisor of moderately large group of workers engaged in production of seedlings and transplants for reforestation or production of ornamental trees and shrubs.

Education and Experience: Graduation from high school and two years experience in forest tree nursery work.

Salary Range: $6,000—$7,800.

Excerpts from an actual state civil service job description for such a position in an Eastern state are as follows:

• • •

EXAMPLES OF WORK PERFORMED:

Participates and supervises helpers in production of forest planting stock by directing the preparation of seedbeds, seeding, weeding, cultivating, watering, pruning and other cultural practices.

Supervises the lifting, counting and grading of all seedlings or transplants shipped from the nursery.

Supervises the gathering and processing of forest tree seed.

Supervises planting and care of cover crops.

Participates and supervises maintenance and construction of nursery buildings, grounds and equipment.

Performs related work as required.

REQUIRED KNOWLEDGES, SKILLS AND ABILITIES:

Knowledge of the techniques and procedures used in the operation of forest tree nursery.

Knowledge of the principles and practices involved in planting, seeding and other nursery work.

Knowledge of, and skill in the use of tools and equipment used in nursery work.

Ability to keep simple records.

Ability to perform manual work.

• • •

Forest Technician

Performs a variety of technical forestry assignments such as timber sales, fire prevention, insect and disease control and forest tree nursery development.

Education and Experience: Graduation from a college with an associate degree in forest technology, certificate from ranger or forestry school, or three years education in forest management from a recognized college.

Salary Range: $6,000—$8,000.

Excerpts from an actual state civil service job description for such a position in an Eastern state are as follows:

• • •

EXAMPLES OF WORK PERFORMED:

Assists in the examination and marking of trees in order to make volumetric computations; assists in the marking of timber for removal from state lands, special use lands, and privately owned lands.

Supervises the construction and maintenance of roads, trails, boundary lines, fire lanes, and buildings.

Reports fires by radio-telephone; recruits, trains, and supervises forest fire wardens and fire crews; submits fire reports when fires are extinguished and conducts investigations to determine causes of forest fires.

Assists in and supervises the production of forest planting stock; supervises seedbed preparation, seeding, weeding, cultivating, lifting, and shipping; and assists in the development and maintenance of seed orchards.

Assists in the control of forest diseases and insects; conducts field surveys and prepares simple maps; prepares and delivers insecticides; and assists in the conduct of experimental projects.

Provides assistance to and exercises control over oil, gas, and mineral operations on state forest lands to insure that the land is maintained or restored to an acceptable state; collects fees for oil and gas operations; collects royalties derived from minerals extracted; and issues receipts and releases.

Maintains time records of laborers and prepares various other reports and records.

Collects fees from the sale of forest products; issues receipts; patrols roads and trails; and enforces state forest rules and regulations.

Assists in advancing the objectives of a forest conservation program by addressing audiences, presenting movies and slides, and distributing posters.

Assists in making surveys and preparing maps of state forest lands.

Performs related work as required.

REQUIRED KNOWLEDGES, SKILLS, AND ABILITIES:
Knowledge of dentrology and forest mensuration.

Knowledge of the methods and techniques of forest protection including fire prevention and suppression.

Knowledge of the conditions that constitute fire hazards.

Some knowledge of land surveying principles.

Some knowledge of algebra and trigonometry.

Some knowledge of the methods, tools, and equipment used in the construction and maintenance of forest facilities, roads, and trails.

Skill in the use of hand tools and power driven equipment utilized in construction and maintenance work.

Skill in the use of surveying and timber estimating instruments.

Ability to learn the laws, rules, and regulations relating to forestry.

Ability to make mathematical computations rapidly and accurately.

Ability to plan, organize, and supervise the work of subordinates.

Ability to keep simple records, analyze data, and prepare written and oral reports.

Ability to establish and maintain effective working relationships with co-workers and the general public.

Sufficient physical stamina to perform strenuous labor particularly in the suppression of forest fires.

• • •

Forest Entomologist

Plans and directs large-scale projects designed to prevent, detect and suppress forest insects.

Education and Experience: Graduation from college with a major in forestry, supplemented by graduate work in forest entomology to level of a Master's degree.

Salary Range: $11,000—$15,000.

MAKING A LIVING IN CONSERVATION

EASY-TO-GET REFERENCES

Career Packet. U. S. Department of Agriculture, Forest Service, Washington, D. C. 20250.

Should You be a Forester? Career Information Service, New York Life Insurance Co., Box 51, Madison Square Station, New York, N. Y. 10010.

So You Want to be a Forester? The American Forestry Association, 919 17th St., N. W., Washington, D. C. 20006.

Careers in Forestry for Women. West Virginia University, Morgantown, W. Va. 26506.

Careers in Forestry. U. S. Government Printing Office, Washington, D. C. 20401. 15¢.

A Job With the Forest Service. U. S. Government Printing Office, Washington, D. C. 20401. 10¢.

Challenge in Wood Research. Misc. Publication No. 1054, U. S. Department of Agriculture, Forest Service, Washington, D. C. 20250.

Forest Service Research. Six-page profile, U. S. Department of Agriculture, Forest Service, Washington, D. C. 20250.

Move Ahead—Research Careers in the Forest Service. Misc. Publication No. 1109, U. S. Department of Agriculture, Forest Service, Washington, D. C. 20250.

Ask any Forester. Society of American Foresters, 1010 16th St., N. W., Washington, D. C. 20036. 10¢.

Career Packet. American Forest Products Industries, 1816 N. St., N. W., Washington, D. C. 20006.

Forester. Career Brief B-52, Careers, Box 135, Largo, Fla. 33540. 35¢.

Forestry Aide. Occupational brief 283. Chronicle Guidance Publications, Moravia, N. Y. 13118. 35¢.

Women in the Forest Service. Division of Personnel Management, Forest Service, U. S. Department of Agriculture, Washington, D. C. 20250.

Employment Outlook for Conservation Occupations: Foresters, Forestry Aides, Range Managers. Bulletin 1550-20, Superintendent of Documents, U. S. Government Printing office, Washington, D. C. 20402. 10¢.

Women in the Forest Service. Misc. Publication No. 1058, U. S. Government Printing Office, Washington, D. C. 20210. 5¢.

Engineers in the Forest Service. Misc. Publications No. 1089, U. S. Government Printing Office, Washington, D. C. 20401. 50¢.

Civil Engineer and Mechanical Engineer. Two-page profiles, U. S. Department of Agriculture, Forest Service, Washington, D. C. 20250.

Employment Outlook for Conservation Occupations: Foresters, Forestry Aides, Range Managers. Bulletin 1550-20, Superintendent of Documents, U. S. Government Printing Office, Washington, D. C. 20402. 10¢.

Range Conservationist. Two-page profile, U. S. Department of Agriculture, Forest Service, Washington, D. C. 20250.

[3]

Working with Wildlife

Wildlife conservation plays an important role in managing the natural resources of this country. It goes far beyond the mere enjoyment of seeing the wild things of the open country and forests for the sake of aesthetic enjoyment. As a recreational asset, hunting, fishing, photography and similar activities are of great economic worth. More basic, an environment that will sustain and foster the wild things of the streams and prairies will also provide a wholesome pattern for human living.

More than 50 million persons hunt or fish in the United States and Canada and millions more travel near and far to see North America's plant and animal life. Trapping produces millions of dollars of annual income, and trains youngsters everywhere in the fundamentals of conservation. Wild animals are a part of the heritage of all people. Some species need protection for they have become scarce through the actions of man. Others are in excess and may cause economic losses to farm or forest crops.

WHAT IS A WILDLIFE CONSERVATIONIST?

A Wildlife Conservationist is a well-educated person who has been trained in the skills that will conserve the nation's wildlife resources. He may formulate and apply scientifically sound solutions to wildlife problems; he may carry out management programs; he may enforce regulations; or he may educate and inform others about wildlife conservation.

A wide choice of careers is available in this field. Wildlife management and research biologists offer basic guidance to many agencies and individuals in all parts of the country and in all types of environment.

Good wildlife management demands a well balanced technical background to enable the biologist to work directly with creatures of the wild and their environment. Refuges, public game areas, marshes, lakes and streams, forests—all must be managed to suit particular needs of the resource.

Research obtains the facts on which good management is based. Taxonomy, physiology, genetics, ecology, disease, nutrition, population dynamics, land use changes, pollution, chemistry, biocides—facts from these and other areas of research are called into play in many investigations. Of late years, wildlife research has become increasingly important in determining the effects on man, himself, of his too liberal use of poisons and pesticides.

Enforcement of laws and regulations is essential. The modern game protector or conservation officer is no longer just a "game warden." He may manage game, take census, control wildlife populations, recommend seasons, and be a year-round educator as well, working continually with the public regarding conservation laws, principles and practices.

PLACES OF EMPLOYMENT

There is need for people trained in wildlife work in such Federal agencies as the Bureau of Sport Fisheries and Wildlife, Forest Service, National Park Service, Bureau of Indian Affairs, Bureau of Land Management, Soil Conservation Service, Army Corps of Engineers, Agricultural Research Service, and National Institute of Health. Most state game and fish departments now employ, in administrative, management, or research capacities, personnel with professional wildlife specialty training.

Colleges and universities offering wildlife training necessarily employ instructors with advanced degrees and practical experience. These institutions usually conduct research requiring highly trained specialists. During the last twenty years or so, private interests have absorbed a number of men trained in wildlife disciplines, mostly at large waterfowl or other hunting clubs, on estates, and in a few industrial laboratories. Commerical interests concerned with wildlife, such as fur establishments and fisheries, have limited staffs of specially qualified persons.

School graduates specializing in wildlife management secure positions about as follows:

State and provincial agencies	65-70 percent
Federal agencies	15-20 percent
Educational institutions	5-10 percent
Private agencies or individuals	2-5 percent

QUALIFICATIONS AND CAREER OPPORTUNITIES

In general, a college education is essential for almost all wildlife occupations. Communication skills, particularly good speaking and writing abilities, must be a vital part of the training.

Most wildlife resource and conservation problems relate to people. Therefore, in addition to a thorough education in physical and biological sciences, training in such subjects as English, languages, history, culture, religion, geography, statistics, and the economics of food and fiber production is useful.

The Wildlife Society recommends as minimum course credits for a Bachelor's degree, 30 semester hours in biological sciences, including at least six hours in courses related to understanding or manipulation of environments, at least six hours in vertebrate biology and classification; at least nine hours in botany and related plant sciences and a minimum of 15 semester hours in at least two sciences such as chemistry, physics, mathematics, soils, or geology. Most universities and colleges offer such courses in biological sciences as a normal part of their curricula.

Graduate work is almost essential for research or some of the broader phases of management and administrative work or teaching.

Wildlife biology and management, while providing many opportunities for a satisfying life, also demand extras not required in many other fields of endeavor. A mere love for the outdoors is not enough, although helpful. Duties of a wildlife biologist may require outdoor activity of an arduous nature, sometimes in remote areas.

Physical difficulties and other conditions in the field make the employment of women impractical in many wildlife conservation jobs. But women do find wildlife employment successfully in many of the laboratory research, information, education, or interpretive positions.

EMPLOYMENT OUTLOOK

The majority of wildlife conservation positions are with state, provincial and Federal agencies. Such positions usually are under civil service, requiring entrance examinations and at least a Bachelor's degree for positions such as Wildlife Biologist, Game Manager, Park Naturalist, Research Biologist, and Conservation Officer.

State or provincial agencies include departments of conservation, natural resources, fish and game, forestry, or parks and recreation. Federal agencies include, in the United States, the Fish and Wildlife Service, Forest Service, National Park Service, Bureau of Land Management, Bureau of Outdoor Recreation, Soil Conservation Service, Armed Forces branches, and the Public Health Service; and in Canada, the Wildlife Service, Park Service, and the Department of Fisheries.

Career oportunities also exist in private research laboratories, numerous scientifically-based foundations, museums, community nature or conservation centers, zoos, and a growing number of other private and public conservation organizations throughout the world.

POSITIONS IN THE WILDLIFE PROFESSION

Workers in this field are generally employed as administrators, directing programs concerned with conservation and management; they include Wildlife Area and Refuge Managers, and Wildlife Biologists, who determine biological facts and procedures useful to guiding various programs in the conservation and management of wildlife.

In all but a few state departments, administration of wildlife resources includes sport fisheries. At the Federal level, the Bureau of Sport Fisheries and Wildlife administers both.

A few typical job descriptions are:

Biologist 1

This is the beginning-level professional work as an assistant in a fish and game area or on a research project.

Education and Experience: Graduation from an acceptable four-year college with specializations in fisheries or wildlife, or both.

Salary Range: $7,000—$9,000.

Biologist 2

At this level, the employee may be responsible for one or several aspects of a fish and wildlife program, managing an area or carrying out research on a specific fish or wildlife species.

As Wildlife Area Manager, employee supervises management of a designated area. A Wildlife Biologist studies plant and animal ecology. A Fisheries Biologist conducts aquatic research studies.

Education and Experience: Graduation from four-year college with specialization in fisheries or wildlife. One year full-time paid experience in field, or one-year graduate training as substitute.

Salary Range: $7,500—$9,500.

Biologist 3

Advanced professional work on district, project or research level required in areas as described above for Biologist 2.

Education and Experience: Graduation from acceptable college. Three years paid experience. Graduate training, substitute one year.

Salary Range: $7,500—$10,000.

Excerpts from an actual state civil service job description for such a position in a Midwestern state are as follows: • • •

EXAMPLES OF WORK

Wildlife Area Manager:

Plans, supervises and participates in the development, maintenance and management of a designated fish and game area.

Supervises the construction of hunting and fishing facilities, provide information, and sells licenses and collects fees.

Wildlife Biologist:

Plans and conducts studies on plant and animal ecology.

Conducts wildlife census.

Secures cooperation of landowners in developing wildlife habitat.

Inventories and evaluates prospective hunting and fishing lands in various counties.

Fisheries Biologist:

Conducts aquatic research studies.

Prepares an inventory of fish population in state owned waters and recommends proper fish management procedures.

Renovates and restocks fish in state waters.

Advise private lake owners on proper management.

General (applicable to all Biologist III):

Plans and develops operating budgets.

Prepares and delivers talks to sportsmen and civic groups on the work of the Division.

Writes progress reports and articles for publication.

Performs related work as assigned.

REQUIREMENTS FOR WORK

Wildlife Area Manager:

Extensive knowledge of methods and practices utilized in wildlife management and in the development of hunting and fishing activities.

Extensive knowledge of the principles of the life cycles of wildlife in the state.

Ability to supervise construction and agricultural activities and the care of such equipment.

Fisheries and Wildlife Biologist:

Extensive knowledge of the principles and practices of animal and plant ecology.

Extensive knowledge of research methods and practices employed in the laboratory and field.

Extensive knowledge of the ecology, identification, and classification of fish and/or wildlife in the state.

Ability to plan and participate in field surveys and laboratory work.

General (applicable to all Biologist III):

Ability to plan, schedule, assign, and supervise the work of others.

Ability to organize and record technical data and to present technical reports.

Ability to prepare and deliver talks to interested groups.

• • •

Biologist 4

Responsible supervisory work in management, development and maintenance of small area. Works independently, but his work is subject to review.

Education and Experience: College graduation. Three years paid experience.

Graduate training, substitute one year.

Salary Range: $9,000—$11,000.

Biologist 5

Supervisory conservation work with state or region-wide responsibility for research projects, management districts, fish and game areas, wildlife refuges, hatcheries, license sales and general management.

Education and Experience: College graduation. Three years paid experience. Graduate training, substitute one year.
Salary Range: $9,500—$12,000.

Biologist 6

High-level administrative work responsible for coordination of an entire divisional program, such as research, management, development, or maintenance of fish and wildlife areas. Works independently, his work subject to general review by an agency or program director.

Education and Experience: College graduate, as above. Five year's experience. Graduate training, substitute two years.
Salary Range: $11,000—$14,000.

Biologist 7

Highly responsible administrative work, directing fish and game activities of a state conservation program. Employee makes responsible, independent decisions, but matters of general policy are determined through conference with National Resources Director.

Education and Experience: College graduation. Eight full years paid experience. Graduate training, substitute two years.
Salary Range: $13,000—$17,000.

Waterfowl Management Agent

A technical position of a specialized nature. Locates suitable area for flooding and planting of suitable aquatics. May involve several areas. Must have good knowledge of aquatic biology.

Education and Experience: College degree in biology or related science. Two year's experience in wildlife management or research.
Salary Range: $8,500—$11,500.

Excerpts from an actual state civil service job description for such a position in an Eastern state are as follows:
• • •

EXAMPLES OF WORK PERFORMED:

Prepares waterfowl management and development plans; selects lands suitable for waterfowl development; submits plans for approval to conservation director and Federal officials.

Supervises preparation of land and planting of waterfowl food crops on non-agricultural lands. Supervises rearing, banding, and release of limited numbers of wildfowl annually.

Makes wildlife counts of ducks and geese on project areas by airplane, truck, boat, and on foot.

Contacts hunters during hunting season to obtain data on the total number of birds killed and other game data.

Performs related work as required.

Required Knowledge, Skills And Abilities:
Thorough knowledge of habits of waterfowl, especially with regard to preferences as to food and habitat.

Considerable knowledge of the principles and practices of wildlife management.

Knowledge of general farming practices and techniques involved in clearing and preparing land for planting;

Knowledge of contractual and related legal processes.

Ability to plan and administer a wildlife conservation program.

Ability to plan and supervise the work of a small group of subordinate personnel.

Sufficient physical strength and stamina to permit the performance of routine farming tasks.

• • •

Game Farm Superintendent

Manages a small game farm. Supervises breeding, hatching, raising and caring for pheasants, quail, ducks and partridges. Oversees farming operations to provide food and pasture, checks disease and controls predators.

Education and Experience: Eighth-grade school education, minimum. Four year's experience in propagation, feeding and care of birds.

Salary Range: $8,000—$10,500.

Excerpts from an actual state civil service job description for such a position in an Eastern state are as follows:

• • •

Examples Of Work Performed:
Supervises game propagators of several grades and laborers in breeding, hatching, raising and caring for game birds.

Supervises operator of incubators, hatchers, brooders and other propagation equipment.

Arranges for farming schedules to be carried out at the proper time and supervises all farming operations.

Supervises the construction and maintenance of game farm buildings and equipment.

Keeps constantly alert for signs of disease or sickness among the game birds being raised and treats ordinary ailments or refers unusual symptons to a superior.

Keeps records and reports of game farm activities.

Patrols premises to control predators.

Performs related work as required.

Required Knowledges, Skills And Abilities:
Considerable knowledge of game farm operations and techniques and the ability to apply this knowledge to operations.

Knowledge of the life habits and requirements of game birds.

Knowledge of and skill in the use of specialized hatchery equipment.

Some knowledge of common game bird diseases and methods of treatment.

Skill in the operation of equipment used in farm operations and game propagation, including farm tools and equipment, incubators, brooders, hatchers and egg candling devices.

Ability to coordinate and supervise the work of a group of subordinates and to train them in proper work methods.

Ability to supervise the operation and repair of hatchery and farming equipment.

Ability to make reports and keep records.

• • •

EASY-TO-GET REFERENCES

A Wildlife Conservation Career for You. S-176, The Wildlife Society, 3900 Wisconsin Ave., N.W., Washington, D.C. 20016.

"Careers in Fish and Game Management." (reprint) *The Conservationist*, June-July, 1964, New York Dept. of Conservation, Albany, N.Y. 12226.

Training and Empolyment of Wildlife Biologists and Fisheries Biologists. *Journal of Wildlife Management*, Vol. 25, No. 2, April, 1961.

Thirty Years of Cooperative Wildlife Research Units. Bureau of Sport Fisheries and Wildlife, Resource Publication Number 6, Government Printing Office, Washington, D.C. 20402.

A Wildlife Management Career in the Forest Service. Two-page profile, U.S. Department of Agriculture, Forest Service, Washington, D.C. 20250.

Careers in Wildlife Conservation. Conservation Department, Olin Industries, East Alton, Ill. 62024.

Wildlife Specialist. Career Brief B-107, Careers, Box 135, Largo, Fla. 33540. 35¢.

Careers for Women in Conservation. Leaflet No. 50, U. S. Department of Labor, Women's Bureau, Washington, D.C. 20240. 10¢

Source List for Careers in the Biological Sciences. American Institute of Biological Sciences, 3900 Wisconsin Ave., N.W., Washington, D.C. 20016.

[4]

Fisheries—
An Expanding Field

Fishing is one of the oldest occupations in the world, with records dating back to 2000 B.C. The Bible is replete with references and parables referring to fish and fishermen. Man has depended upon this product of the sea since the beginning of civilization.

Yet, little is known about what causes changes in great populations of ocean fish life. A trip along the mid-Atlantic coast will reveal huge menhaden processing plants, now idle and falling into decay because these prolific members of the herring tribe have almost vanished. The once-productive pilchards or sardines in California have followed the same pattern. Once famous whitefish and lake trout of the Great Lakes are now a rarity. Pacific salmon catches are but a shadow of their former abundance. Why? The fishery scientist is supposed to answer that question.

Commercial fisheries off the Atlantic and Pacific Coasts that know no man-made political lines must be considered a continent-wide resource. Canadian commercial fishing nets about $160,000,000 and the United States $500,000,000 per year. Thirty-three million U. S. sport fishermen spend well over three billion dollars, while Canadians spend 200 million dollars annually. Fishing, indeed, is big business in both countries.

WHAT FISHERY SPECIALISTS DO

Fishery jobs at the professional level include:

Research into the environment of fish, including the related factors of soil, forests, pollution and the dredging and filling of estuarine environments.

Management programs designed to supplement, maintain or restore fish populations for recreational or commercial purposes, including population and environmental controls, the formulation of catch estimates, and reclamation of fishing waters.

Fish hatcheries, commercial fish farms and related activities are operated largely for the recreational industry.

Teachers are located in at least 107 universities and colleges in the United States and Canada, where courses in fishery science are conducted.

Fisheries specialists cover a wide range of subjects dealing with fresh and salt water species. There is a demand for skills in physiology, nutrition, statistics, population dynamics, ecology, limnology and oceanography.

With the increased emphasis on environmental improvement, this field has a promising future.

PLACES OF EMPLOYMENT

Prior to the reorganization plan which created the National Oceanic and Atmospheric Administration in the Department of Commerce, both Federal fishery agencies were located in the Department of the Interior. Now, the Bureau of Commerical Fisheries has moved to the Department of Commerce while the Bureau of Sport Fisheries and Wildlife remains in Interior. These two Federal bureaus employ most of the scientists in this field.

Other Federal agencies which employ fisheries personnel, although in limited numbers, are the Forest Service, Soil Conservation Service, National Park Service, Water Pollution Control Administration, Corps of Engineers, United States Department of Defense, and the Atomic Energy Commission. In addition, the Food and Agriculture Organization of the United Nations employs fisheries personnel.

Agencies of the various states employ the greatest number of fisheries scientists. They also employ conservation officers to enforce their respective laws.

Colleges, universities and a few large high schools employ fisheries scientists as researchers, teachers and writers.

Collectively, there are many opportunities with private enterprise hydro-power companies, private timber companies, industries with large land holdings, private fish hatcheries, sport club fisheries, city and county recreation departments, agricultural experiment stations, bait farms, and handlers and producers of tropical fish. A few private biological consulting firms and conservation organizations hire fisheries scientists.

Due to the outdoor working conditions and necessity of handling heavy gear, employment of women tends to be limited. However, there are increasing numbers of laboratory and office jobs available to women in both state and Federal agencies.

QUALIFICATIONS AND CAREER OPPORTUNITIES

Enjoyment of the out-of-doors and interest in people as well as in aquatic life are helpful in fisheries careers.

Many fisheries biologists spend much of their time outdoors in varied weather conditions handling fishing gear, boats, motors, and other equipment. Sometimes, the comforts of home are lacking in marine work, often for extended periods.

Correct work and study habits and success in school subjects, especially the sciences, math, and English both written and spoken—are essential.

The fisheries manager, administrator, officer, or teacher works constantly with other people. Public relations and public education are increasingly important aspects of the work.

EMPLOYMENT OUTLOOK

The field of fisheries science is small and young, but it is growing steadily. It offers variety and strong challenge because it is a relatively unexploited science. Commercial fisheries interests see an expanding future for fish farming and harvesting techniques, especially in the under-developed countries of the world.

The new emphasis on environmental studies and actions to halt pollution worldwide will demand fishery scientists in a broad range of specialties.

Many positions involve considerable time in the field during certain special seasons of the year. Marine positions usually require that some time be spent at sea in small vessels. Commercial fisheries are mostly centered on major off-shore fishing banks, but also include work on several inland areas, particularly very large lakes and reservoirs. Teaching positions in universities include classroom, laboratory, and field work. Sport fisheries are located on inland waters and coastal and estuarine waters.

FISHERY POSITIONS

There are two principal categories in the fishery field. Professional and scientific studies establish biological facts, principles, methods and techniques for the management of aquatic resources. These go beyond concern merely for fish alone. They include crustaceous, mollusks—the entire food chain and the total environment. Fish hatcheries operated largely for sport fishermen require the application of methods and techniques dealing with propagation, rearing and stocking of food and game fish. Here, full professional knowledge in the broad field of fishery biology is not essential.

Fishery jobs are distributed among state and Federal agencies, and private industry. All fifty states have fishery operations. At the Federal level, numerous treaties govern the management of commercial fisheries in international waters.

A few typical job descriptions follow:

Fish Hatcheryman 1

As a journeyman fish hatchery worker, the employee engages in all phases of culture pertaining to the care and handling of fish, and maintenance of attendant buildings, grounds and equipment. Such jobs involve work under the direction of a fish hatcheryman of higher pay-grade.

Education and Experience: One year of fish hatchery experience or two years of college with major course work in biology.

Salary Range: $6,500—$7,200.

Excerpts from an actual state civil service job description for such a position in a Western state are as follows: • • •

EXAMPLES OF WORK

1. Records data such as amounts and times of feeding, fish loss in ponds, or water temperature on work sheets.

2. Assists in the treatment of fish for disease by reporting to a supervisor unusual behavior of fish being raised and placing designated chemicals in the water as indicated by the supervisor.

3. Feeds fish as indicated in a feeding schedule, obtaining feed from stockroom, weighing out amounts, distributing feed to ponds. Deviates from schedule if feed is not being consumed and reports deviations to superior.

4. Cleans ponds, removes dead fish and maintains appropriate water flow.

5. Participates in spawning operation by selecting mature fish, removing eggs and sperm, placing fertilized eggs in containers in the hatchery.

6. Performs duties associated with transfer or transporting and liberating of fingerling or adult fish in tank trucks or directly from the hatchery.

7. Participates in the maintenance of the hatchery and related areas by assisting in the care of the grounds and performing such carpentry, plumbing, electrical and mechanical work as is needed to maintain the hatchery and equipment.

8. Assists visitors to the hatchery by answering questions concerning hatchery activities, conducting tours of the hatchery area, and related activities.

9. Assists in training of lower level employees.

RECRUITING REQUIREMENTS, KNOWLEDGE, SKILL AND ABILITY

Knowledge of methods, equipment and supplies used in maintenance of buildings, grounds and equipment; knowledge of fish species and habits; ability to use fundamental mathematics and to read and record accurately; ability to follow oral and written instructions; ability to detect signs of nutrition or disease problems; ability to perform strenuous physical labor.

• • •

Fish Hatchery Manager 1

Usually supervises a small hatchery station or serves as an assistant supervisor of a large station. Must have good knowledge of fish culture operations and techniques, knowledge of life cycles of fish being propagated and reared, and know how to apply techniques toward the objectives assigned the station.

Education and Experience: Associate degree in fishery or wildlife science. Three years of fish hatchery experience, at least one year of which has been in a supervisory position.

Salary Range: $7,500—$9,500.

Fish Liberator

Operates heavy tank truck in transporting fish from hatcheries to designated points of liberation in streams and lakes. Must have thorough knowledge of laws governing operation of trucks on all kinds of roads, the ability to make emergency repairs of equipment and to care for the fish in transit.

Education and Experience: Graduation from senior high school. Two years experience in fish hatchery operations, including operation of a heavy truck.

Salary Range: $7,000—$8,000.

Excerpts from an actual state civil service job description for such a position in a Western state are as follows: • • •

EXAMPLES OF PRINCIPAL DUTIES

1. Stocks lakes, streams, or reservoirs from pre-arranged schedules; arranges for assistance if needed at stocking site; assists in loading at hatchery; ascertains that truck and tank are in proper operating order.

2. Keeps constant check during journey on temperature, oxygen, and operation of aeration system and corrects deficiencies; makes periodic checks on condition of fish and the aeration apparatus within tank.

3. Releases fish according to approved procedure.

4. Prepares reports relative to the distribution of fish and notifies various agencies of action taken.

5. Makes emergency repairs and performs general maintenance on all equipment during non-stocking periods; fabricates liberation equipment including tanks and aeration apparatus.

RECRUITING REQUIREMENTS, KNOWLEDGE, SKILL AND ABILITY

Thorough knowledge of the state laws pertaining to the operation of motor vehicles upon the highways; extensive knowledge of the location and physical characteristics of the state's game waters; considerable knowledge of fish culture operations and techniques; considerable knowledge of the life habits and requirements of the state's game species of adult fish, fish eggs and fish fry; ability to keep records and write reports; ability to make satisfactory public contacts and to give information such as explanation of work operations to organized sports groups and others; ability to make general and emergency repairs to motor equipment.

• • •

Aquatic Research Supervisor 1

Has independent responsibility for a broad phase of commercial fisheries research. Analyzes research data, directs research programs, represents higher authority in public meetings, recommends regulatory actions and speaks for his agency in meetings at state, Federal and international levels.

Education and Experience: Master's degree in fisheries biology. Three year's experience with commercial fisheries.

Salary Range: $11,500—$15,000.

Aquatic Research Supervisor 2

Duties similar but more responsible than Aquatic Research Supervisor 1. Directs program for entire state or region. Policy reviewed by Federal Regional or State Director. Requires greater administrative and public relations abilities.

Education and Experience: College degree in fisheries or related biological science. Five years responsible field and research experience in commercial fish management.

Salary Range: $13,500—$17,000.

Aquatic Biologist 1

Assists in scientific fisheries research and management studies in fish population, nutrition and environment. Works on technical details of research projects and as experience is gained to more complex segments of research projects.

Education and Experience: Graduation from four-year college with specialization in fisheries biology or related science.

Salary Range: $7,000—$9,000.

Aquatic Biologist 2

Basic duties similar to Aquatic Biologist 1, but supervises greater area. Responsible for research projects on disease, nutrition, etc., on all activities in a geographical area. Has considerable independence of action.

Education and Experience: College graduate in fisheries or related science. Four years progressively responsible field and research experience in fishery management.

Salary Range: $10,000—$12,000.

Aquatic Biologist 3

State or region-wide responsibility for an aquatic biological research program, supervising stream rehabilitation, fish stocking or other broad programs, or directing major research operations. Develops plans in both biological and administrative aspects.

Education and Experience: College degree in fisheries or related science. Five years responsible field and research experience.

Salary Range: $11,000—$14,500.

Fishery Biologist 1

This is a beginning grade in the fishery research series. Employee makes surveys as basis for measuring present and potential values of areas for fish populations, conducts studies on growth rates, collects fish for analysis, records sex and weight, takes scales for aging, and collects plankton and bottom food supplies.

Education: High school graduate.

Salary Range: $6,500—$8,500.

Fishery Biologist 2 (Commercial)

This is a second-level professional trainee who assists research biologists of higher pay-grade in performance of highly complex biological assignments. Work involves marine spawning grounds, installation and operation of anadromous fish counting weirs, conducting spawning surveys, or obtaining ecological and biological marine data.

Education and Experience: College degree. One year professional experience.
Salary Range: $8,000—$10,500.

Biologist, Fish and Wildlife

A Federal class in the program of assessing the effects of water use developments on fish and wildlife resources. Requires close liaison with Federal agencies such as Corps of Engineers, Reclamation Service, Soil Conservation Service and private power companies. Requires, in addition to fish and wildlife, a good knowledge of engineering, agriculture, soils and applicable laws for a region encompassing several states.

Education and Experience: College training in fisheries or wildlife. Three years professional experience. Graduate studies may be substituted for experience.
Salary Range: $12,000—$15,500.

Stream Improvement Foreman

Conducts operations to clear streams of debris and obstructions to permit passage of fish during various seasons of the year. This may involve fishways, low head dams and other small structures. Supervises laborers and inspects and passes on work done by contractors. Structures consist of concrete and rock and earth fills.

Education and Experience: High school. Three years experience in heavy construction, including use of explosives, or fishway inspection and operation.
Salary Range: $7,500—$9,500.

Excerpts from an actual state civil service job description for such a position in a Western state are as follows:

• • •

EXAMPLES OF WORK

1. Supervises or inspects varied phases of construction work required in erection of fishways, such as construction of concrete forms, rock and earth moving, steel reinforcing, pouring concrete and erecting small buildings.

2. Supervises or inspects stream and channel clearance projects.

3. Plans and lays out jobs from drawings, specifications and sketches; assigns work to construction crew members.

4. Assists supervisory engineers in planning new construction, remodeling and repair constructing work; and requisitions materials, supplies and equipment.

5. Works with crew on various phases of the job including rock and earth removing, form and steel work construction, operating such equipment as concrete mixers, jackhammers, and bulldozers.

6. Inspects contract work involving stream and channel clearance.

7. Checks plans and work progress with supervisors, maintains records of personnel, materials and labor costs, and prepares progress reports.

8. Contacts land owners to obtain permits or easements for access to streams.

9. Operates and inspects fishways.

RECRUITING REQUIREMENTS, KNOWLEDGE, SKILL AND ABILITY

Thorough knowledge of practices, tools, equipment and materials used in general construction work; thorough knowledge of the use and maintenance of heavy equipment; knowledge of the handling and use of explosives, some knowledge of engineering principles as applied to control of water flow and construction of concrete work; skill in estimating, planning, laying out and supervising general construction work; ability to read and interpret drawings, sketches and specifications; ability to estimate personnel, materials, and equipment necessary for jobs; ability to keep simple records and make reports.

•   •   •

EASY-TO-GET REFERENCES

Fisheries as a Profession. American Fisheries Society, 1040 Washington Building, Washington, D. C. 20005.

"Training and Employment of Wildlife Biologists and Fisheries Biologists." *Journal of Wildlife Management*, Vol. 25, No. 2, April 1961.

Employment Opportunities in the Bureau of Sport Fisheries and Wildlife. National Wildlife Federation, 1412 16th St., N.W., Washington, D. C. 20036.

Fisheries Scientist (Fish Cultivist). Chronicle Guidance Publications, Inc., Moravia, N. Y. 13118. 35¢.

Careers in Biology. American Institute of Biological Sciences, 3900 Wisconsin Ave., N.W., Washington, D. C. 20016.

Biologist. Occupational Brief 344, Chronicle Guidance Publications, Moravia, N. Y. 13118. 35¢.

[5]

Oceanography

The ocean, which covers more than two-thirds of the earth's surface, provides valuable foods and minerals, influences the weather, serves as a "highway" for transportation, and offers many varieties of recreation. Oceanographers study the ocean—its characteristics, movements, physical properties, and plant and animal life. The results of their studies not only extend basic scientific knowledge, but contribute to the development of practical methods for use in operations such as forecasting weather, improving fisheries, mining ocean resources, and defending the nation.

NATURE OF OCEANOGRAPHY WORK

Oceanographers plan extensive tests and observational programs and conduct detailed surveys and experiments to obtain information about the ocean. They may collect and study data on the ocean's tides, currents, and waves; its temperature, density, and acoustical properties; its sediments; its subbottom; its shape; its interaction with the atmosphere; and marine plants and animals. They analyze the samples, specimens, and data collected, often using electronic computers. To present the results of their studies, they prepare maps and charts, tabulations, reports, and manuals, and write papers for scientific journals.

In developing and carrying out tests and observational programs, oceanographers use the principles and techniques of the natural sciences, mathematics, and engineering. They use a variety of special instruments and devices that measure the earth's magnetic and gravity fields, the speed of sound traveling through water, the oceans' depths, the flow of heat from the earth's interior, and the temperature and chemical composition of the water.

Specially developed cameras using strong lights enable oceanographers to photograph marine organisms and the ocean floor; new research vehicles transport marine scientists to the floor of the sea. When their work requires new oceanographic instruments or analytical techniques, they usually develop them.

SPECIALTIES IN OCEANOGRAPHY

Most oceanographers are specialists in one of the branches of the profession. *Biological oceanographers* (marine biologists) study the ocean's plant and animal life and the environmental conditions affecting them. *Physical oceanographers* (Physicists and geophysicists) study the physical properties of the ocean, such as its density, temperature, and ability to transmit light and sound; the movements of the sea; and the relationship between the sea and the atmosphere.

Geological oceanographers (marine geologists) study the topographic features, rocks, and sediments of the ocean floor. *Chemical oceanographers* investigate the chemical composition of ocean water and sediments, and chemical reactions that occur in the sea. *Marine meteorologists* study the interaction of the atmosphere and the ocean, and the processes by which weather over the ocean is generated. *Oceanographic engineers* and *electronic specialists* design and build the systems, devices, and instruments used in oceanographic research and operations.

WHO EMPLOYS THEM

About 3 out of 4 oceanographers are engaged primarily in performing or administering research and development activities. A number of oceanographers teach in colleges and universities; a few are engaged in technical writing, consulting, and in the administration of activities other than research.

SCIENCE OF THE SEA

Studies of the ocean must largely be carried out at sea, from surface vessels and submersibles. In recent years, very specialized oceanographic vessels have been developed by several branches of government and by research institutions such as the Woods Hole Oceanographic Institute and the Scripps Institute of Oceanography.

All of these research vessels need to be stationed at the right place in the sea at the right time. Therefore, scientific navigation and precision positioning is required. Trained captains, navigators and specialized crews are needed in addition to the scientific staff aboard.

Oceanic research is complex. The configuration of the oceanic basins and that of their dependent seas calls upon the science of hydrography including the sounding of ocean depths to determine bottom compositions and contours for submarine navigation, ocean mining and related purposes. This study, like navigation, includes studies which encompass astronomy and cartogrophy. Hydrographers arc principally data collectors and compilers. Most are employed by government agencies.

Closely connected with the configuration of the oceanic basins is the study of the nature and structure of the basin —studies largely geological in character. The geologist, however, is confronted with more than the general formation of the sea basin. He must also consider bottom sediments which can be analyzed best by a chemist, a physicist, and a marine biologist.

The study of sea water itself is another great area of inquiry. Chemical composition and physical characteristics at various latitudes, longitudes and depth are important. Since the sea covers more than two-thirds of the earth's surface and extends in some areas to depths of several miles, the determination of its ever-changing chemical and physical properties are matters of considerable magnitude and require many chemists and physicists.

The waters of the sea are never at rest. Waves, currents, tides, and flow are intimately related to movements of the moon, the sun and the rotation of the earth, so astronomical considerations are involved.

Meteorology and climatology encompass a great group of oceanic problems. Covering, as it does, the greater part of the earth's surface, the sea plays a profound part in making the earth livable. The sea has been aptly called the "Thermostat of the World." The Gulf Stream brings a warming effect to Western and Southern Europe. The Japanese current warms our Pacific Coast from the equator to the Gulf of Alaska.

Finally, the sea is the home of a great variety of plant and animal life, calculated by experts to support at least 500,000 distinct species of plants and animals from the unicellular plant to the whale. The very origin of our life seems definitely connected with the sea.

Thus, life in the sea offers a host of problems to the botanist and the geologist as well as to the mathemetician studying the population dynamics of food fishes and mammals. As almost all the food eaten by man derives from living matter, the study as well as the full and wise exploitation of sea plants and animals for human food will almost surely increase in importance as man, himself, continues to increase in numbers.

Thus, the study of oceanography encompasses almost every discipline in the scientific spectrum. Career possibilities in this field are almost limitless.

POSITION REQUIREMENTS AND SOME TYPICAL POSITIONS

The study of oceanography requires, first of all, ocean-going research vessels, equipped to perform numerous scientific tasks, supplemented by onshore laboratories where water samples and aquatic specimens may be analyzed, identified and catalogued.

First of all and absolutely basic is the requirement that employees must be willing to live and work at sea harmoniously and in close relationship with crew members and research staff. Those in major positions must be immune from chronic sea sickness. Life on the ocean is exacting in its demands.

A few summaries of the wide variety of skills required are:

a. For operations—

Ship's Master

Has full responsibility for all matters pertaining to the operation and administration of a vessel, 750 gross tons or over; supervision and discipline of crew; navigation, safety and material condition of the vessel. Maintains ship's log in accordance with accepted maritime practices, records all diving and towing operations; responsible for planning, loading and stowing scientific equipment and articles of a similar nature. Works with scientific personnel in planning and execution of necessary research work.

Required Knowledge and Skills:

Knowledge of laws, rules and regulations pertaining to navigation; ship's machinery; crew supervision and discipline; skill in obtaining, storing and care of food, equipment and supplies.

Education and Experience: One year's service as Chief Mate of oceanic motor vessel of 1000 gross tons or more. Possession of valid U.S. Coast Guard License equal to Master of Ocean Motor Vessels; endorsed as Radar Observer. Salary Range: $14,000—$16,500.

Ship's Chief Engineer

Operates and maintains marine diesel engines and auxiliary mechanical and electrical equipment used in ocean motor vessels of at least 1000 horsepower; responsible for economical and efficient operation and maintenance of engineering department. The Chief Engineer is supervised by the Master in regard to speed, manoeuvers and other aspects of operation of the oceanographic research vessel.

Required Knowledge and Skills:

Knowledge of and ability to operate diesel engines of at least 500 horsepower; plan major alterations to meet changing needs of research project; ability to think and act quickly in emergencies.

Experience: One year's service as first assistant engineer of motor vessels, possession of a valid U.S. Coast Guard License equal to Chief Engineer, Motor Vessels, 1000 horsepower or over. Salary Range: $13,500—$15,500.

Port Engineer

Installs, maintains and repairs diesel engines and auxiliary equipment at shore-based installation and in relief capacity on ocean motor vessels of at least 1000 horsepower. When required to go to sea on a research vessel, usually on short notice, he assumes the duties of the Chief Engineer, First, Second or Third Assistant Engineer, as required.

Work examples include operating and maintaining shore-based lathes, drill presses and other apparatus; supervising operation of marine diesel engines on a research vessel in response to signals from the bridge; maintaining and repairing engines, electrical equipment, hydraulic machinery, refrigeration equipment and related apparatus.

Required Knowledge and Skills:

Extensive knowledge of his profession; one year's experience as first assistant engineer of motor vessels; possession of a valid U.S. Coast Guard license equal to Chief Engineer, Motor Vessels, 1000 horsepower or over.

Salary Range: $10,500—$13,500.

Boatswain

Supervises deck maintenance and operation; responsible for planning detailed schedule of the order in which work will be performed; anchoring, mooring and unmooring of ship. Must work in close cooperation with research and student personnel and insure that they comply with all appropriate rules of good seamanship while on deck; assists researchers by maintaining proper operation of research gear and tackle.

Required Knowledge and Skills:

Knowledge of methods, materials and maintenance work; navigation rules pertaining to area of operations; ability to meet emergency situations.

Experience and Training: One year's service on deck of vessels of 100 gross tons or over, while certified by the U.S. Coast Guard at a level equal to Able Seaman Any Waters, Unlimited.

Salary Range: $6,500—$7,500.

b. Technical positions—

Marine Technician

At sea, collects physical oceanographic, biological, geological and geophysical data by making Nansen bottle casts to collect water samples and temperatures; reads deep-sea reversing thermometers to determine water temperatures at various depths; records surface synoptic weather and bathythermographic observations; operates electronic equipment towed from an ocean-going vessel for the purpose of obtaining a continuous record of surface temperatures and currents; operates echo-sounding equipment; collects and preserves plankton samples and fish specimens, which involve net-towing, night-light dip-netting and other methods.

At shore-based laboratories or at sea, processes temperature and salinity observations to calculate movements of ocean currents; analyzes reversing thermometer readings, manipulates graphs and scales; plots and draws curves of vertical distributions of temperatures, salinity, oxygen, and phosphate-phosphorus content; computes densities and draws charts of currents; operates automatic filtrating machines.

Maintains, repairs and calibrates scientific equipment and uses advanced electronic sampling and data processing devices.

Marine technicians are usually trained to perform multidisciplinary duties in the fields of physical oceanography, biology, geology, geophysics, chemistry, and data processing. Basic requirements include ability to work under adverse conditions, willingness to spend up to 150 days a year at sea, accuracy and interest in the collection of data, and ability to get along with people. To qualify, all must have a B.A. or B.S. degree, or experience and/or training in chemical, biological or data processing fields.

A typical marine research organization includes:

Marine Technician I

Works under close supervision and instruction as trainee, acquiring familiarity with data collection and processing and chemical analysis techniques.
Salary Range: $6,000—$8,500.

Marine Technician II

Has completed two years of "on-the-job" training, acquired theoretical and practical experience and is expected to perform with considerable freedom but is subject to review by senior technician.
Salary Range: $7,000—$9,500.

Senior Marine Technician

Functions with a great degree of independence, receiving project assignments from a supervisor and reporting results upon their completion. Submits new designs and improvements of equipment used at sea, and reports on equipment tests. Assists in training new technicians.
Salary Range: $8,000—$11,000.

Marine Technician Supervisor

Plans, coordinates, supervises and evaluates the activities of a marine technician group; sets up training programs and improves data collection and processing precedures; acts as Field Party Chief at sea.
Salary Range: $9,000—$12,000.

c. For communications work—

Ship's Radio Officer

Installs, operates, tests and repairs electronic apparatus aboard a research ocean motor vessel, involving navigation gear, radar, radio and other related equipment.
Requirements:
Other than thorough knowledge of radio and electronic theory and equipment, such as radar, sonor, loran, oscilloscope, thermistors, etc.; must have physical capacity to perform arduous duties involved, willingness to work and live at sea for long periods of time; immunity from chronic seasickness, ability to work and live harmoniously in close relationship with crew members and research staff.

Experience and Training. High school graduation and two years experience as a licensed marine radio operator.
Salary Range: $8,750—$10,000.

Ship's Cook-Steward

Purchases, prepares and serves food aboard ship.

Excerpts from an actual crew member's state civil service job description as listed by a Western state are as follows:

* * *

EXAMPLES OF WORK:
1. Prepares and serves breakfast, lunch, dinner, and other meals as may be required.
2. Makes up menus, considering anticipated number of diners, food-stuffs on hand, popularity of dishes and recent menus, dietetic principles, holidays, and cooking time needed, either independently or in conference with the captain or project supervisor.
3. Bakes bread, rolls, muffins, and biscuits; cuts, bones, and trims and prepares meats; makes soups, sauces, dressings, and salads.
4. Serves food and beverages to staff, guests, and crew; cleans tables; sets up for meals and cleans tables and dining room after meals are completed.
5. Washes and cleans utensils and equipment.
6. Cares for living quarters, cleaning rooms and making beds; launders sheets and clothing, mending as required; replenishes paper supplies, and maintains first aid supplies.

RECRUITING REQUIREMENTS KNOWLEDGE, SKILL AND ABILITY:
Thorough knowledge of the principles, procurement, preparation, cooking, and including baking and serving of food; thorough knowledge of galley and dining area sanitation and safety measures used in the operation, cleaning, and care of utensils, equipment, and work areas; thorough knowledge of food handling sanitation; wide knowledge of food values as well as nutritional and economical substitutions with food groups, and the types of food required on long sea voyages; skill in the preparation and cooking of all food groups and ability to use appropriate equipment; skill in judging food quality; ability to determine food quantities necessary for groups of varying size; ability to instruct and work with assistants; ability to keep records; high standards of cleanliness; willingness to live and work at sea for long periods of time; physical capacity to perform the arduous duties involved and ability to obtain a U. S. Health Service Food Handler's Certificate; immunity from chronic sea sickness; ability to work and live in close relationship with crew members and research staff.

Experience and Training: Graduation from senior high school and two years of full-time paid experience as a cook including at least six months on a vessel; or a satisfactory equivalent combination of experience and training.

Salary Range: $7,000—$8,400.

* * *

EASY-TO-GET REFERENCES

Career Opportunities in Biology. Russell B. Stevens, National Academy of Sciences, Washington, D. C. 20418.

(Continued—next page.)

MAKING A LIVING IN CONSERVATION

Careers in Marine Science. FAO Fish. Tech. Paper 90 (1969), Food and Agriculture Organization of the United Nations.

Biochemist. Career Brief B 101, Careers, Box 135, Largo, Fla. 33540. 20 ¢

Biochemist. Occupational Brief 132, Chronicle Guidance Publications, Moravia, N. Y. 13118. 35 ¢

The Sphere of the Geological Scientists. Chalmer J. Roy, American Geological Institute, 1444 N St., N.W., Washington, D. C. 20005.

Those Alluring Careers in Ocean Sciences. Changing Times, The Kiplinger Magazine. April, 1970.

Geology—Science and Profession. American Geological Institute, 1444 N St., N.W., Washington, D. C. 20006.

[6]

Positions in
Park Administration

The United States is a leader among nations in preserving in a natural
and unspoiled condition her great areas of national significance that have
natural, scientific, and historic values. These areas compose the National Park
System. There are in addition, of course, also numerous state and even county
parks within America.

The National Park Service was created in 1916. It was charged with the responsibility for maintaining the national parks, monuments, and similar reservations
for the inspiration and enjoyment of this and future generations. The organic
legislation manifests a challenging purpose for the parks: "To conserve the scenery
and the natural and historic objects and wildlife therein, and to provide for the
enjoyment of the same in such manner and by such means as shall leave them
unimpaired for the enjoyment of future generations."

OUR NATIONAL PARK SYSTEM

The National Park System is not a static institution, however. With each Congres-
sional enactment, it has taken on new vitality in response to the needs of our
growing population: To preserve natural beauty; to protect places of scientific
interest; to interpret our historic heritage; and to provide healthful outdoor recreational opportunities—these also are its goals.

A part of the Department of the Interior, the National Park Service has six
regional offices, three planning and service centers and 259 field areas located in
the United States, Puerto Rico and the Virgin Islands.

There is a wide range of locations and kinds of installations. Every state has one or more. Designations include National Parks, Monuments, Lakeshores, Seashores, Historical Parks, Scenic Riverways, Military Parks, Battlefields, Historic Sites, Recreation Areas, Memorials, Cemeteries, Parkways, Scientific Reserves, International Parks, and Historic and Natural Landmarks. Total land ownership is about 23-1/3 million acres. This compares, for instance, with a total area equivalent to the state of Indiana, which has 23-1/2 million acres.

All states and territories have state parks as well as other recreational facilities. In addition, there are a growing number of counties and local political subdivisions that develop and manage various parks and other recreational facilities.

The Bureau of Outdoor Recreation estimates that demands on publicly-owned areas have been increasing at the rate of more than ten percent per year since 1960, and that by the year 2000, demands will be four times greater than it was in 1965.

The Land and Water Conservation Fund Act of 1965 provides funds for Federal land use agencies and, on a 50-50 matching basis, for the states. During the first 4-1/2 years of the fund's existence, ending June 30, 1969, the National Park Service, the Forest Service, and the Bureau of Sport Fisheries and Wildlife had received 254.9 million dollars. The states received 241 million dollars in matching funds for more than 4,000 widely diversified projects.

Recent state emphasis has been slanted toward recreation developments such as swimming pools, public beaches, boat launching ramps and other facilities which bring outdoor recreational opportunities closer to large centers of population.

Bond issues have been a recent major source of financing state and local outdoor recreation programs. New highs in bond issues for recreation, recorded in Alabama, Connecticut, Florida, Maryland, Maine, Massachusetts, Michigan, New Jersey, Ohio, Pennsylvania, Tennessee, Texas, Washington and Wisconsin, totaled some 1.4 billion dollars.

Public recreational developments at all levels fail to keep pace with burgeoning demand. Yosemite National Park has had air pollution problems from too many sociable evening campfires. Yellowstone has experienced miles-long traffic jams caused by enthusiastic watchers-of-the-bears.

In many areas, local pollution problems caused by wastes from recreational boats have closed public bathing beaches. Everywhere, the pressure on public recreational facilities is intense.

PLACES OF EMPLOYMENT

Employment opportunities exist nationwide. Some are on National Parks, some state, some county and some local. All require staffing. All need people with various required degrees of competence and training.

QUALIFICATIONS AND CAREER OPPORTUNITIES

Federal Park Rangers are represented at the entrance level at grade GS 5, their jobs progressing to GS 15. A Ranger may develop into a Supervisory Park Ranger, Staff Specialist, Interpretive Specialist or other such position.

As the Ranger's career progresses in the field of park management, he will be involved with programming, planning, supervising and instituting new management programs and practices. He may progress into positions such as Superintendent, Regional Director, or rate other management jobs. Generally, the higher positions are filled with experienced people from the ranks.

Park Naturalists perform scientific and professional work dealing with the natural history programs of the Service. Much of this work centers on the interpretation to the visiting public of natural history features of areas in the System; the study, research, management, and protection of these areas; and curatorial tasks related to exhibits and reference collections. Interpretive duties include meeting the public; conducting guided trips; planning, preparing, and delivering illustrated talks both in areas administered by the Service and in nearby communities; planning and developing museums and exhibits; and writing for publication.

Park Aide jobs are first steps to careers as Park Technicians. Through on-the-job experience, Park Aides develop their skills and knowledge of practical park operations. Aides work at the more basic tasks involved in fire fighting, conservation programs, providing information to the public, enforcing the law, operating campgrounds, and other jobs related to park and recreation area operation.

Park Technicians perform a wide variety of functions, usually following the direction or plans for Park Rangers. They work on fire fighting crews, and conservation teams working on soil erosion, plant and insect control projects.

In historic and archeological areas, Technicians carry out plans to preserve and restore buildings and sites. They operate campgrounds, including such tasks as assigning sites, replenishing firewood, performing safety inspections, and providing information to visitors.

Technicians lead guided tours and give talks to groups of visitors. They also operate projectors and sound equipment for slide shows and movies. Technicians direct traffic; go on road patrols, operate radio dispatch stations and perform other law enforcement and public functions.

Women may not be employed as Park Rangers because of the rugged, and sometimes hazardous nature of the duties. However, employment opportunities for women exist in Park Specialist positions, and in interpretive positions such as Park Naturalist, Historian, Archeologist, and Park Guide.

State organizational structures pretty well follow the general pattern described above.

EMPLOYMENT OUTLOOK

Interior's *Manpower In The Sixties* report showed an increase for the decade in Park Service employees of almost 47 percent. Even so, this agency has been unable to keep abreast of the demands. A restless people, with more leisure time on their hands, new luxurious trailers, and an urge to travel, are crowding parks—national, state and local—as never before.

PARK POSITIONS

Positions in this profession vary widely, just as the needs of the recreational public differ from area to area and among age and income groups.

No simple listing of positions can cover all conditions, but a few samples will illustrate the broad pattern of outdoor recreation in America served by the local, state and Federal park systems and the fundamental employee qualifications.

Here they are:

Federal Park Ranger, GS 5

The entrance or beginning trainee level designed to train and give on-the-job experience to park rangers, aid quick learning of methods, practices and techniques in park management practices and agency policies, philosophies and procedures. Duties involve habitat and disease investigations, fish stocking, surveys, visitor contact, law enforcement and minor administration functions.

> Education and Experience: Graduation from four-year college with majors in park and recreation management or related sciences, or three years acceptable experience.
> Salary Range: $7,000—$9,000.

Federal Park Ranger—GS 9

A more advanced position in the Ranger series. Here, the Ranger makes field surveys of forest, range and wildlife management, forest and insect disease control, fire hazards, drafts guidelines for law enforcement, rescue services, campgrounds, trails.

> Education and Experience: College degree and 2 years professional experience, or Master's degree.
> Salary Range: $10,500—$13,500.

Federal Park Ranger—GS 11

At regional and national levels, this grade includes planning and developing long-range management objectives dealing with visitor loads, wildlife management, soil erosion, protection of historic structures, fire hazards, etc. Contacting public officials, negotiating agreements, resolving complaints and reconciling conflicting public viewpoints.

> Education and Experience: College degree as outlined for GS 5. Three years professional experience. Two years graduate study as a substitute acceptable.
> Salary Range: $12,600—$16,500.

Federal Park Ranger—GS 13

Duties at regional and national levels, extensive in application. Must have expert knowledge of basic law, conservation principles, and fundamental park philosophies. Must assert leadership, provide staff coordination, review major programs of park managers and rangers.

> Education and Experience: Ph.D. degree or equivalent; minimum of 3 years experience.
> Salary Range: $17,750—$23,100.

Park Aides

These are first steps to careers as Park Technicians. Through on-the-job experience, Park Aides develop their skills and knowledge of practical park operations.

Tasks may involve fire fighting, conservation programs, law enforcement, campground operation and a wide variety of other duties. A number of these jobs are *seasonal*.

Education and Experience: High school or higher education.

Salary Range: $5,000—$6,000.

Excerpts from an actual state civil service job description for such a position in a Western state are as follows: • • •

DISTINGUISHING FEATURES OF WORK

Appointments to the class of Park Aide are made on a seasonal basis; employment normally extends from late spring through late summer. Under the direct supervision of a Park Manager or Park Ranger, the employee assists in maintaining cleanliness and order in the park or parks; provides park information and directions to the public; collects and tabulates fees; keeps records of park use; periodically checks supplies and replenishes depleted stocks; and assists Park Rangers and maintenance personnel in making minor repairs or park improvements. Work in this class is distinguished by the variety of semi-skilled clerical and custodial tasks peculiar to park operations, and by the seasonal characteristics.

EXAMPLES OF WORK

1. Informs the visiting public on facilities available, park rules and regulations, park flora and fauna, historical data and related information.

2. Assists permanent park staff with routine maintenance and repair of park grounds, equipment, and structures.

3. Collects fees for park use.

4. Makes periodic reports, accounts for money collected, submits requisitions for supplies.

5. Cleans rest-rooms and other park buildings and replenishes supplies.

RECRUITING REQUIREMENTS, KNOWLEDGE, SKILL AND ABILITY

Working knowledge of the state's animal and plant life; working knowledge of the history and geography of the park and immediate vicinity; ability to meet and deal with the public effectively; ability to give information regarding park rules and facilities and to look after the comfort and safety of visitors.

• • •

Park Technicians

Perform a wide variety of functions dealing with fire fighting, conservation, soil erosion, plant and insect control. In certain areas, carry out plans to preserve and restore buildings and grounds and provide information to visitors.

Education and Experience: At least two years college, plus experience in studies related to park operations.

Salary Range: $6,200—$10,000.

Park Managers

Direct the overall operations of a park, park area, region, or other important organizational unit of a park system. They oversee, control and guide the use of personnel, funds, materials and the facilities needed to complete various park improvement or renovation programs and carry out important public relations functions for the park organization.

Education and Experience: Full 4-year course in an accredited college or university with BS degree in one or more subjects oriented toward natural science, history, archeology, police science, recreation or closely related courses. At least three years experience for higher grades.

Federal Salary Range: $10,500—$24,000.

Park Guides

Give talks, answer questions, conduct groups of visitors through area, and give general information concerning area or facility. Some positions are temporary; women may qualify for some positions.

Education and Experience: Written examination.

Federal Salary Range: $7,000—$9,000.

Seasonal Park Positions

Uniformed seasonal Park Rangers, Ranger-Naturalists, Ranger Historians and Ranger-Archeologists meet and talk with millions of visitors to areas in the National Park System. Women may qualify for some positions.

Education and Experience: Two years experience or 2-1/2 years college. Personality and ability to meet and deal with people. Minimum age 18 years.

Federal Salary Range: $6,000—$8,000 annual rate, plus overtime above 40 hours per week.

Other Federal Positions

Numerous related positions are: Editorial and Information Specialists, Technicians, Exhibit and Museum Specialists, Curators, Biologists, Geologists, Foresters, Forest Rangers, and Park Police, at various grades and with a wide range in salary.

State Park Specialist 1

Training position for a newly-employed graduate with a degree in any science related to park management. Works in preliminary phases of park or recreation development, involving general technical and administrative tasks, under supervision.

Education and Experience: College degree in park management, forestry, landscape architecture, biological science, physical education or recreation.

Salary Range: $7,200—$9,000.

Excerpts from an actual state civil service job description for such a position in a Midwestern state are as follows:

• • •

KIND OF WORK

This is the training position for a newly employed college graduate. Employee works under the supervision of an experienced park or recreation area manager. Employee is responsible for working in the preliminary phases of park or recreation area development, and for general supervision of activities. Work may consist of general duties or of duties assigned in a specific state park or recreation area, and involves general technical and administrative tasks. Employee works under supervision to secure desired results, subject to review and approval by the park or recreation area manager and an administrative official.

EXAMPLES OF WORK (*Illustrative only*)

Supervises employees in operation of recreation facilities such as a bathing beach, bathhouse, campground, boat dock, etc.

Responsible for handling of state funds and preparation of reports and records.

Prepares requisitions for supplies, tools, materials and equipment.

Ascertains that equipment receives proper care, instructs employees in respective duties and maintains property in good order.

Supervises maintenance and construction as required.

REQUIREMENTS FOR WORK

Basic knowledge of professional park and recreation area management and principles.

Ability to establish and maintain harmonious working relationships with the general public and co-workers; to supervise operation of a segment of the recreation program at a park or recreation area.

Ability to prepare and present talks to interested groups.

Ability to maintain required records and to prepare essential reports.

• • •

State Park Specialist 5

Responsible, professional work in developing and supervising state park operations, working independently, but work subject to review by higher authority.

Education and Experience: College degree as outlined for Park Specialist 1.

Three years field experience, with substitution for graduate training.

Salary Range: $9,500—$12,000.

State Park Ranger 1

The *Park Ranger 1* performs a variety of semi-skilled tasks, operates equipment used in the maintenance, repair and improvement of state parks and wayside facilities, assists park visitors by providing information and directions; does related work as required.

Under the supervision of a senior Park Ranger or Park Manager, the employee performs the permanent maintenance of park and wayside buildings, grounds, resources, utilities and services provided to park and wayside visitors. His work is distinguished from other semi-skilled occupations by the combination of manual tasks, frequent and meaningful public contact, and a wide variety of work assignments. He may occasionally be assigned to more complex work or equipment to gain experience and training or may perform other tasks related to work requiring a lesser degree of skill.

• • •

EXAMPLES OF WORK

1. Performs a variety of semi-skilled tasks in the repair, construction and maintenance of buildings, tables, stoves, rest rooms, water and sewer systems, footpaths, etc.

2. Meets the public as required, registers visitors and assigns camp spaces,

55

gives information on facilities available, park rules and regulations, historical data and related information.

3. Operates light dump or other types of truck and comparable equipment.

4. Patrols park for detection of fires and protection of natural features; plants and controls vegetation; enforces park rules and regulations.

RECRUITING REQUIREMENTS, KNOWLEDGE, SKILL AND ABILITY

Knowledge of the safe operation of tools and equipment and the precautions to be taken in order to avoid accidents; knowledge of the methods and materials used in the maintenance of buildings, grounds and park facilities and in the servicing of automotive equipment; knowledge of the history of the park and the animal and plant life found in the park; knowledge of first aid practices; ability to meet the public effectively, to give information regarding park rules and facilities, and to promote the safety and welfare of park visitors; and the ability to enforce park regulations; ability to do heavy manual labor and to work outside in all types of weather; ability to follow oral or written instructions.

> Education And Experience: Graduation from a senior high school, preferably with six months experience in work relating to the care and maintenance of buildings and grounds, operation of mechanized equipment; or a satisfactory equivalent combination of experience and training.
> Salary Range: $6,500—$7,000.

· · ·

State Park Foreman

Directs small work crews in construction or maintenance projects at a large state park or supervises all activities at a small park.

> Education and Experience: Two years experience in park operations.
> High school graduation.
> Salary Range: $6,000—$8,000.

State Park Superintendent 1

Beginning-level professional work in operation and maintenance of state park and recreational facilities. Work is performed under supervision of a senior professional.

> Education and Experience: Bachelor's degree in forestry, outdoor recreation, park planning or management, engineering or appropriate natural science. Two years experience.
> Salary Range: $7,500—$9,500.

State Nature Preserve Director

Directs and plans a state-wide system of designated nature preserves; responsible for selection, evaluation, development, operation and maintenance of nature preserves. Works under direction of State Director of Parks and Memorials.

> Education and Experience: Acceptable college degree. Eight full years experience. Graduate training may be substituted for two years experience.
> Salary Range: $9,500—$12,000.

Excerpts from an actual state civil service job description for such a position in a Midwestern state are as follows:

• • •

EXAMPLES OF WORK (*Illustrative only*)

Evaluates sites of unique natural significance recommended for registration.

Evaluates sites proposed for dedication as nature preserves.

Prepares, for submission to the Natural Resources Commission, terms of dedication for sites recommended to become nature preserves.

Prepares comprehensive acquisition and operating budgets and programs for nature preserves and provides administrative supervision of their operation.

Prepares and recommends the adoption of criteria for evaluation of proposed nature preserves.

Prepares requisitions for the purchase of supplies, materials, and equipment.

Prepares publications on nature preserves.

Prepares annual reports, annual and biennial budgets, and drafts of legislation pertinent to the Nature Preserves System.

Represents the Nature Preserves System in meetings with other state and federal agencies, and educational groups interested in establishment and preservation of natural areas.

Performs related work as assigned.

REQUIREMENTS FOR WORK

Extensive knowledge of the principles and practices involved in the administration of natural areas.

Extensive knowledge of the statutes, rules, and administrative precedents governing the establishment and operation of a Nature Preserves System.

Extensive knowledge of the programs, facilities, features, and operating characteristics of the Nature Preserves System.

Extensive knowledge of current developments, literature, and sources of information concerning Nature Preserves administration.

Extensive knowledge of the botanical, biological, and geological significance of natural areas.

Extensive knowledge of plant and animal taxonomy.

Ability to plan, assign, and preserve the work of others.

Ability to evaluate proposed areas as to their desirability for development as nature preserves.

Ability to express one's self clearly and concisely, orally, and in writing, and to conduct effective public relations.

Extensive knowledge of the principles, practices and equipment of general office management.

• • •

EASY-TO-GET REFERENCES

Careers in the National Park Service. U. S. Department of the Interior, National Park Service, Washington, D. C. 20240.

Career Packet. Bureau of Outdoor Recreation, Department of the Interior, Washington, D. C. 20240.

"*Careers in Outdoor Recreation.*" (reprint) *The Conservationist.* New York Department of Conservation, Albany, N. Y. 12226.

Working for the Bureau of Outdoor Recreation. Bureau of Outdoor Recreation, U. S. Department of the Interior, Washington, D. C. 20240.

[7]

The Soil Conservationist Field

Soil conservationists supply farmers, ranchers, and others with technical assistance in planning, applying, and maintaining measures and structural improvements for soil and water conservation on individual holdings, groups of holdings, or on watersheds. Farmers and other land managers use this technical assistance in making adjustments in land use; protecting land against soil deterioration; rebuilding eroded and depleted soils; stabilizing runoff and sediment-producing areas; improving cover on crop, forest, pasture, range, and wildlife lands; conserving water for farm and ranch use and reducing damage from flood water and sediment; and in draining or irrigating farms or ranches.

NATURE OF THE WORK

The types of technical services provided by soil conservationists are as follows: Maps presenting inventories of soil, water, vegetation, and other details essential in conservation planning and application; information on the proper land utilization and the treatment suitable for the planned use of each field or part of the farm or ranch, groups of farms or ranches, or entire watersheds; and estimates of the relative cost of, and expected returns from, various alternatives of land use and treatment.

After the landowner or operator decides upon a conservation program that provides for the land to be used within its capability and treated according to the planned use, the conservationist records the relevant facts as part of a plan which, together with the maps and other supplemental information, forms a program of action for conservation farming or ranching. The soil conservationist then gives the land manager technical guidance in applying and maintaining the conservation practices.

WHERE EMPLOYED

Most soil conservationists are employed by the Federal Government, mainly by the U.S. Department of Agriculture's Soil Conservation Service and the Bureau of Indian Affairs in the Department of the Interior. Some are employed by colleges and state and local governments; others work for banks and public utilities.

TRAINING AND ADVANCEMENT

A Bachelor of Science degree and a major in soil conservation or a related agricultural science constitute the minimum requirement for professional soil conservationists. Those who have unusual aptitude in the various phases of the work have good chances of advancement to higher salaried technical administrative jobs.

EMPLOYMENT OUTLOOK

Employment opportunities for well-trained soil conservationists have been good in recent years. Opportunities in the profession will expand because government agencies, public utility companies, banks, and other organizations are becoming interested in conservation and are adding conservationists to their staffs. Other new openings will occur in college teaching, particularly at the undergraduate level. In addition, some openings will arise because of the normal turnover in personnel.

ABOUT SOIL CONSERVATION POSITIONS

Soil conservationists usually have a broad range of duties dealing with coordinated programs of soil and water conservation which require the application of a wide range of agricultural sciences.

Soil Conservation Technicians supervise non-professional, technical and specialized workers in the general field.

Together, they perform public services at Federal, state, and local levels which cover conservation tasks, such as conducting snow surveys in the West to forecast municipal and irrigation water supplies; planning farm ponds on public and private lands to furnish water for livestock, wildlife and recreation; identifying the need and examining proposals for dams on larger watersheds for flood control, agriculture, domestic and industrial use; planting grasses and trees in the semi-arid West to control dust storms and sand dunes; and restore vegetation to strip-mined and other devasted land areas.

Under basic law and philosophy, soil improvement programs are accomplished through local landowner-organized, controlled and administered Soil Conservation Districts.

A few typical jobs at this basic organization level follow:

Soil Conservation Field Representative

Professional work dealing with organization and development of local soil conservation districts and allied programs in cooperation with local, state and Federal participating agencies.

Education and Experience: Bachelor's degree with major in soil conservation.
Two years experience in application of soil conservation practices.
Salary Range: $8,500—$11,500.

Excerpts from an actual state civil service job description for such a position in an Eastern state are as follows: • • •

EXAMPLES OF WORK PERFORMED

Attends soil conservation district meetings advising on program development, budget planning and availability of technical services through participating agencies.

Provides training to district directors, cooperating agency personnel and other interested groups in the objectives, operations, policies and procedures of the state soil conservation program.

Consults with county commissioners and local organizations for the purpose of promoting the formation and development of new soil conservation districts.

Participates in examinations of watershed areas to determine watershed development and flood prevention needs.

Represents the State Soil Conservation Commission in the promotion and development of solid conservation practices among land owners in the various conservation districts.

Prepares reports on district activities, writes conservation articles for local distribution, and lectures to urban and rural groups on the benefits of soil conservation practices.

Performs related work as required.

REQUIRED KNOWLEDGES, SKILLS AND ABILITIES

Considerable knowledge of agricultural land capabilities and the conservation methods and techniques required to keep land permanently and profitably productive.

Knowledge of the basic disciplines relating to agricultural conservation including agronomy, agricultural engineering, agricultural economics, geology and forestry.

Knowledge of the programs and objectives of participating agencies interested in providing technical conservation services.

Ability to promote and develop leadership in district conservation programs.

Ability to establish and maintain effective working relationships with local officials, farmers and other related organizations.

Ability to express ideas clearly and effectively, orally and in writing.

Ability to speak effectively in public. • • •

Soil Conservation Program Specialist

Professional soil conservation work associated with planning and development of specialized activities within a state conservation program, coordinating state technical conservation activities such as watershed development, flood prevention, soil surveys, fish and wildlife development, range rehabilitation.

Education and Experience: Bachelor's degree in soil conservation. Four years experience in soil conservation or a related discipline.

Salary Range: $9,500—$12,500.

Excerpts from an actual state civil service job description for such a position in an Eastern state are as follows: • • •

EXAMPLES OF WORK PERFORMED

Plans, develops and coordinates the State Soil Conservation Commission's participation in specialized conservation activities such as watershed development, flood prevention or soil survey projects.

Conducts preliminary investigations of proposed specialized conservation projects and prepares technical recommendations consolidating the view of the State Soil Conservation Commission.

Attends district soil conservation meetings integrating specialized conservation activities with local projects.

Assists local organizations in the performance of their obligations incurred as a participant in specialized conservation activities such as watershed development, flood prevention or soil survey projects.

Supervises the distribution of state aid to local districts for specialized soil conservation activities.

Prepares reports on specialized projects, writes articles for publication and lectures to interested groups on the benefits of specialized conservation practices.

Performs related work as required.

REQUIRED KNOWLEDGES, SKILLS AND ABILITIES

Thorough knowledge of agricultural land capabilities and the conservation methods and techniques required to keep the land permanently and profitably productive.

Considerable knowledge of the basic disciplines relating to agricultural conservation including agronomy, agricultural engineering, agricultural economics, geology and forestry with particular emphasis on their relationships to specialized conservation activities such as watershed development, flood prevention or soil surveys.

Knowledge of the objectives and specialized programs of farm organizations and related participating agencies interested in providing technical conservation services.

Ability to plan and coordinate a specialized conservation activity among several levels of government.

Ability to establish and maintain effective working relationships with local, state and Federal officials and other interested groups.

Ability to express ideas clearly and effectively, orally and in writing.

Ability to speak effectively in public.

• • •

Soils Engineer

Performs a variety of engineering duties in the sampling, analysis and design of soils used in construction of water management engineering for erosion control, range management, wildlife recreation and related activities.

Education and Experience: Bachelor's degree in civil or mining engineering, or geology. Four years experience in related field.

Salary Range: $9,000—$11,000.

Excerpts from an actual state civil service job description for an *entry-level* soils engineer in an Eastern state are as follows:

• • •

EXAMPLES OF WORK PERFORMED

Assists a higher level engineer in field investigations, survey and profile review, and research projects.

Inspects and maintains controls on soil construction.

Supervises augering and drilling operations.

Classifies a wide variety of soils using field survey, auger, and core-drilling information.

Performs related work as required.

REQUIRED KNOWLEDGES, SKILLS, AND ABILITIES

Knowledge of the earth's strata and geological structure with particular emphasis on the state's native soils, their composition, and structure.

Knowledge of soil mechanics design and testing.

Knowledge of the engineering principles and practices applied in the location, design, and construction of roads, dams, and comparable structures.

Knowledge of mathematics sufficient to perform moderately complex algebraic computations.

Knowledge of basic physics.

Ability to interpret soil profiled, maps, and construction plans.

Ability to prepare clear and concise engineering reports.

• • •

EASY-TO-GET REFERENCES

"Careers in Soil and Water Conservation." (reprint) *The Conservationist*, Oct.-Nov., 1963, New York Department of Conservation, Albany, N. Y. 12226.

Your Career in ASCS. U. S. Department of Agriculture, Agricultural Stabilization and Conservation Service, Washington, D. C. 20250.

Careers in the Soil Conservation Service. Four booklets: "Students Start Your Career in SCS Before You Graduate" (MP No. 714), 5¢; "An Engineering Career for You in the Soil Conservation Service" (MP No. 715), 10¢; "A Soil Science Career for You in SCS" (MP No. 716), 10¢; "Careers in Soil Conservation Service" (MP No. 717), 10¢. All four publications are available from the U. S. Government Printing Office, Washington, D. C. 20402.

Soil Conservationist. Chronicle Guidance Publications, Inc., Moravia, N. Y. 13118. 35¢.

Soil Scientist. Chronicle Guidance Publications, Inc., Moravia, N. Y. 13118. 35¢.

Careers in Conservation. Soil Conservation Society of America, 7515 N. E. Ankeny Road, Ankeny, Iowa 50021.

[8]

Challenging Positions in the Environmental Health Field

Out-of-doors jobs are no longer confined to forestry, recreation, hunting
and fishing. Now they encompass the broad field of the environment.
Man's notoriously careless and destructive actions are finally bringing on serious
national and international concern for his own well-being. Some go so far as to
call it a crisis for "survival."

POLLUTION, WATER AND OTHER NATIONAL PROBLEMS

Lake Erie is classed biologically as "dead." Areas on many streams, rivers and
lakes are described today by official signs "Polluted", "Unsafe", "Do Not
Drink", or "Dangerous." Fish kills have become standard barometers for water
quality. Queries such as "if a fish can't live in it, do you want your youngster to
swim in it?" have brought the message home to the masses. Restrictions on auto
use in centers of population—New York, Los Angeles, Tokyo—during periods
of heavy smog; daily weather reports including "Air Stagnation Areas;" all have
awakened the public as never before in history.

New laws, regulations and policies are being enacted at all levels of government.
Federally, the Environmental Protection Agency and the National Oceanic and
Atmospheric Administration have recently been established. Statewise, a dozen
states, among them the most populous in the country, have created Environmental
Commissions. Privately, several groups have formed organizations which have

successfully curtailed the ocean dumping of unwanted oil and gas wastes. Others have succeeded in drastically reducing the use of poisonous DDT, mercury and other agricultural and commercial by-products. Practices of many private companies and official agencies are being successfully challenged.

POSITION DESCRIPTIONS

Because of the broad significance of this field, embracing as it does many talents and professional skills, only a few positions are described. All are typical state positions.

Water Treatment Plant Supervisor

Skilled, minor supervisory work in operation of an institutional water treatment plant, where water supplies are treated and tested for turbidity, alkalinity, chlorine residual and other factors affecting potability and purity.

Education and Experience: High school or vocational school. Three years experience in water treatment plant operation.

Salary Range: $7,000—$9,000.

Geographer

Responsible for systematic exploration, identification, analysis and interpretation of physical and geographic features of the earth's surface. Data used to analyze effects of movement and distribution of populations in relation to water supplies, industry and related factors in a given area.

Experience and Training: Master's degree in geography. Two years responsible experience in field.

Salary Range: $10,500—$14,000.

Mine Drainage Engineer

Professional engineering work, making inspections of mining installations and operations to ascertain compliance with state laws dealing with mine drainage. Collects water samples, investigates pollution of public and private waters by drainage wastes, their effects upon stream sanitation and methods for their abatement and reduction.

Education and Experience: Four years college with a major in mining, civil engineering, or geology.

Salary Range: $6,500—$8,500.

Open Pit Mine Conservation Inspector

Responsible for technical inspection and enforcement of applicable state mining laws which require operators to control untreated drainage waters and mine waters which flow into public streams contrary to conservation principles.

Education and Experience: High school graduate. Four years practical experience in open pit mining and conservation.

Salary Range: $9,500—$13,000.

Chemist 1

Performs professional work in the examination and analysis of chemical substances to evaluate air, water and food substances and determine the degree of their contamination and suitability for human use. May be required to testify in various hearings or in court on results of findings.

Education and Experience: Bachelor's degree in chemistry. Two years laboratory experience.
Salary Range: $8,500—$11,000.

Water Quality Chemist

Professional position in field of water supply and pollution control, as advisor to Sanitary Water Board on pollution control and water chemistry; coordinates findings with other states, arranges for research grants, helps develop legislation concerning water pollution control and water conservation.

Education Experience: Ph.D. in chemistry, chemical engineering or closely related field. Three years experience.
Salary Range: $13,000—$17,000.

Ground Water Geologist

Conducts professional work in field, investigates state-wide water pollution control, advises State Sanitary Water Board, assists in preparation of corrective legislation, supervises laboratories conducting investigations in ground water problems.

Education Experience: College graduate in geology. Three years experience.
Salary Range: $14,000—$19,000.

Director Air Pollution Control

Administrative professional work directing statewide air pollution control as part of general environmental health service program. Involves goals, policies, legislation, research and technical decisions. High level of competence required to enlighten general public on air pollution engineering hazards.

Education and Experience: Bachelor's degree in chemical, civil industrial, mechanical or electrical engineering. Nine years responsible experience in field of air pollution control.
Salary Range: $19,000—$25,000.

Public Health Trainees

Various states have positions for Public Health Trainees, the jobs being identified under various names; i.e. - Environmental Health Trainee, Environmental Health Technician I, Public Health Engineering Trainee, etc. Some of the positions are seasonal—summer only—while others represent part-time job opportunities for college students working toward various engineering degrees useful in Public Health or the Environmental Health fields.

In general, these kinds of positions are introductory technical work for students in the field of air pollution control and sanitary engineering, the job emphasis being on inspection and investigative work or projects, all performed under the supervision of a professional superior. The work encompasses making laboratory tests to identify the substances and characteristics indicative of water or air pollution, compiling information relative housing and neighborhood quality, the number and causes of various types of non-highway accidents, etc. These employees are often assigned inspection schedules concerned with industrial hazards and water treatment facilities, inspections and follow-up actions on various complaints, inspections of water supply systems and treatment facilities, sewage collection systems and treatment facilities, etc. They may be called upon to conduct inspections of various streams, bathing places, watersheds, etc. They may also assist in the collection of air samples. Frequently, the employee may be given the opportunity to concentrate in a particular area of interest such as air pollution control or sanitary engineering.

Education and Experience: There is usually a requirement for completion of at least one year in college and that the employee be engaged in a full-time college program working toward one of the several engineering degrees useful in Environmental or Public Health work. This is not always the case, however, as in some of the trainee jobs, the successful completion of a training program in environmental health approved by the employing agency may be substituted. In general, the applicant must have some knowledge of basic general science. College work leading toward a degree in biology, a chemical science or physics is also usually acceptable.

Salary Range: $4,500—$6,000.

Sanitary Engineer I

This is beginning level professional work in sanitary engineering. The employee conducts surveys, performs investigations and inspections of water supply systems and treatment facilities, sewage collection systems and treatment facilities, etc. He is responsible for field laboratory analysis and the preparation of various technical reports, most all of them concerned with the safety and merit of water in various streams, bathing places, watersheds, etc., and the efficacy of sewage disposal and treatment.

Education and Experience: Bachelor's degree in sanitary, public health, chemical or civil engineering including course work in sanitary engineering.

Salary Range: $8,000—$11,000.

EASY-TO-GET REFERENCES

Careers in Resource Management. Branch of Employment and Training, Bureau of Land Management, U. S. Department of the Interior, Washington, D. C. 20240.

"Environmental Education." *Journal of Research and Development in Conservation Communications,* Dumbar Educational Research Services, Inc., Box 1605, Madison, Wisc. 53701.

Your Career and Clean Water for America. U. S. Federal Water Pollution Control Admisistration, Washington, D. C. 20000.

Water Pollution Control Operator. Division of Manpower Development and Training, Office of Education, Department of Health, Education and Welfare, Washington, D. C. 20202.

[6]

Waterways Safety, Game Protection, and Conservation Officer Jobs

Administration of the nation's natural resources brings official agencies in daily contact with a most important, and often difficult element— people. "Please" and "Thank you" signs are helpful and adequate for the vast majority of folks who enjoy the out-of-doors, but there are always a few who recognize only the man with the badge of authority. Various investigative, safety and other area managers are therefore indispensable in any well run conservation organization.

GAME PROTECTORS AND STATE REVENUES

In the field of fisheries and wildlife, the game protector is the backbone of the organization. He is in constant contact with sportsmen, farmers, ranchers and enforcement officers of other agencies, so his observations become the chief basis for the annual regulations. He checks creel and bag limits to see that management regulations are observed by the public. He makes certain that hunting and fishing licenses have been purchased. These constitute the very lifeblood of the state agencies, most of which receive no other revenue. Federal Aid revenues from excise taxes on fishing tackle and arms and ammunition are distributed to the states on the basis of license sales and land and water area. Technicians and others in the state organizations are equally important, but to the vast majority of sportsmen and landowners, the local game protector represents the organization.

VANDALISM, TRAFFIC CONTROL AND BOATING SAFETY

In public parks, traffic control is a major responsibility to afford the widest use to the greatest number of visitors. Here, enforcement officers are a necessity. Vandalism is one of the most serious problems in public parks, where some mischievous persons always persist in defacing signs, breaking up wooden furniture for campfires and dumping their litter indiscriminately everywhere.

In Federal and state forests there are always regulations to govern the cutting of timber, travel into restricted areas by automobiles and, more lately, snowmobiles. Regulations are also necessary relative campsites, livestock grazing and similar uses.

On public streams and lakes, the fast-growing sport of pleasure boating and water skiing creates numerous and often urgent problems. Speed boats can be very dangerous in the hands of inexperienced drivers and they are often a real aggravation to fishermen and other boaters.

Under international treaties with Canada and Mexico, the taking of migratory birds, including ducks and geese is regulated by the Federal government. A corps of game management agents operates in all states and territories working in close cooperation with enforcement officials of the 50 states. Part of the agent's duties is the checking for possession of the Federal Duck Stamp, the proceeds of which finance enforcement, wildlife refuges and research.

PLACES OF EMPLOYMENT

All state conservation departments and practically all Federal land-use agencies.

QUALIFICATIONS AND CAREER OPPORTUNITIES

The tendency is toward the employment of college graduates in all of the more responsible grades, but at lower field levels, graduation from high school is acceptable. Because of the exacting nature of enforcement work—rules of procedure, arrest, evidence in court, etc., a rigorous course of in-service training is necessary before the wearing of a badge is permitted.

Advancement follows a succession of steps from patrolmen and deputy positions to full game protector status. Most Federal officers are recruited from the ranks of state employees.

With the recent emphasis on environmental problems, there should be an expansion in enforcement opportunities.

SOME TYPICAL POSITION DESCRIPTIONS

A few job descriptions to illustrate the general nature of these positions follow:

Conservation Officer Trainee

Introductory conservation work in developing skills and knowledge required in the enforcement of state conservation laws, an enrollee in a State School of Conservation learning game and fish laws, enforcement methods, field procedures, fish, bird and mammal identification, land and water management practices and agency policies.

Education and Experience: Graduation from high school.
Salary Range: $5,500— $6,800.

Conservation Officer 1

Responsible for enforcement of state game and fish laws in an assigned district or implementation of a land and water management area. Work may involve a substantial element of personal danger and demands tactful and courteous treatment of the public and the ability to impart information on the social importance of wildlife conservation. Little direct supervision.

Experience and Training: Graduation from a State Training School.
Salary Range: $7,000—$9,000.

Conservation Protection Supervisor

Administrative conservation work in assisting with state-wide direction of fish and game law enforcement. Supervises activities in absence of chief. Within this general field, requires thorough knowledge of state, Federal and local laws and court procedures.

Experience and Training: Standard high school. Six years of progressively responsible experience in law enforcement.
Salary Range: $10,000—$13,500.

Waterways Patrolman Supervisor

Supervises fish and boating safety law enforcement programs in an assigned region of state. Develops and implements public information and educational program at regional level, conducts in-service training programs and assigns Waterway Patrolmen to districts within the region.

Education and Experience: High school graduation. Two years experience in fish conservation or boating safety work.
Salary Range: $7,500—$10,000.

Excerpts from an actual state civil service job description for such a position in an Eastern state are as follows:

• • •

EXAMPLES OF WORK PERFORMED

Assists in supervising district Waterways Patrolmen engaged in the enforcement of fish and boating safety laws, fish stocking operations, and general maintenance of fisheries conservation standards, in an assigned region.

Supervises and participates in the prosecution of suspected violators of the fish and boating safety laws.

Conducts in-service training programs and assigns Waterways Patrolmen to districts in an assigned region.

Develops and implements a public informational and educational program at the regional level.

Develops course outlines, audio-visual aids, public information booklets, and related materials, and disseminates this information to district Waterways Patrolmen and the public.

Assists in preparing the budget for the region.

Prepares news releases, magazine articles, scripts for broadcasts, and exhibits.

Investigates or supervises the investigation of requests for special licenses or permits; issues special licenses and permits.

Reviews reports submitted by District Waterways Patrolmen to assure conformance with laws, rules, regulations, and state policies.

Prepares reports for submittal to the division supervisor and to the central office.

Performs related work as required.

REQUIRED KNOWLEDGES, SKILLS, AND ABILITIES

Knowledge of the laws, rules, and regulations governing boating, fishing, and hunting in the state.

Knowledge of native fish and aquatic plants and animals, their habits, and natural requirements.

Knowledge of investigational and arresting procedures utilized in the fish conservation and boating safety programs.

Some knowledge of the principles and practices of the investigation of requests for special licenses and permits.

Some knowledge of the principles and practices of effective supervision.

Skill in the use of fishing tackle, boats, and boating equipment.

Ability to enforce laws and regulations with firmness and tact.

Ability to develop and conduct an effective regional in-service training program.

Ability to develop an effective regional public information and educational program.

Ability to prepare news releases, magazine articles, scripts for broadcasts, and exhibits.

Ability to communicate effectively, orally and in writing.

Ability to establish and maintain effective working relationships with associates, subordinates, and the public.

Ability to work long hours under varying climatic conditions.

Willingness to transfer from region to region within the state as required by employer.

• • •

Marine Safety Education Specialist

Teaches specialized education in the field of marine safety through public information media and public training programs, including extensive public speaking appearances.

Education and Experience: High school graduation. Two years paid experice in boat or ship operation, knowledge of state and Federal laws governing registration and operation of watercraft.

Salary Range: $7,000—$9,500.

Excerpts from an actual state civil service job description for such a position in an Eastern state are as follows:

EXAMPLES OF WORK PERFORMED • • •

Develops and presents public marine safety programs to educate both adults and children in the proper and safe utilization of marine equipment.

Plans and develops various marine safety education projects and programs; prepares news releases and other information for eventual publication.

Develops various marine safety courses for presentation to enforcement personnel involved in motor boat patrol work.

Speaks to civic, boating, and other organizations or groups on marine safety; develops promotional material for presentation by the various news media which is designed to stimulate program participation.

Reviews and selects instructional materials and training aids for use in training and education programs.

Coordinates the preparation of boating instructions and other related circulars; ensures that an enforcement manual for motor boat patrol work is adequately maintained.

Prepares various reports; reviews and replies to correspondence.

Performs related work as required.

REQUIRED KNOWLEDGES, SKILLS, AND ABILITIES

Considerable knowledge of the principles and practices of marine safety.

Considerable knowledge of the principles, practices, and media of public relations.

Considerable knowledge of state and Federal boating laws and regulations.

Knowledge of inland waterway navigation principles.

Knowledge of various audio-visual aids available for use in training.

Ability to develop education programs and courses and to select and adapt available materials to meet training needs.

Ability to instruct and lead group discussions and conferences.

Ability to express ideas clearly and effectively, orally and in writing.

Ability to speak effectively in public.

Ability to establish and maintain effective working relationships with boaters, public officials, civic and other interested groups, and the public.

• • •

Federal Game Management Agent

Operates in specified district and establishes liaison with state conservation personnel, court officials, other Federal, state, county and municipal enforcement officials on migratory bird matters. Duties involve enforcement of Federal laws; management, such as banding and population surveys; depredations on agricultural crops by waterfowl, permits and conservation education and training.

Education and Experience: Bachelor's degree in wildlife management.

LL.B or higher degree in recognized law school. Two years experience.

Salary Range: $8,500—$11,250.

Excerpts from an actual U.S. civil service job description for such a position are as follows:

• • •

DUTIES.

The incumbent executes the work program for the sub-district and helps supervise agents detailed to assist in its accomplishment as follows:

71

a. ENFORCEMENT.

He develops and executes a system of coordinated patrols for the prevention, detection, and investigation of law violations and the apprehension of violators; participates as directed by the Regional Office with undercover operators to detect market hunting and other illegal acts; and prepares cases for prosecution and represents the Bureau at court in their prosecution. He develops and maintains a cooperative enforcement program with the State Game Department, military, other Federal and local enforcement agencies. He maintains working relations with U. S. Attorneys and Federal, State, County and municipal court systems in the sub-district.

b. MANAGEMENT.

The incumbent conducts migration studies, banding projects, breeding ground population surveys, nesting studies, harvest surveys, wintering ground population inventories and other field investigations to aid in the management of migratory birds, including summation of the data as directed.

c. DEPREDATIONS CONTROL.

The incumbent plans and conducts migratory game bird depredations control by investigating damage complaints, giving advice on damage control, and demonstrating techniques and devices for abatement of damage to crops or other property. He assists in the development, testing, and evaluation of control devices and methods. He issues scare permits for minimizing migratory bird damage to agricultural crops. He recommends issuance of killing permits when necessary, monitors adherence to permit conditions, and takes appropriate action to correct discrepancies.

d. PERMITS.

Incumbent investigates applications for permits under Migratory Bird Treaty, Bald Eagle and Lacey Acts, and recommends appropriate action by the Regional Office. He advises permittees about their responsibilities and reviews and inspects their activities. He takes necessary action to correct discrepancies.

e. CONSERVATION EDUCATION AND TRAINING.

The incumbent must maintain a balanced public relations program directed toward improving public appreciation and support of conservation programs through personal contact, public appearances, radio, television, the press and correspondence. He participates in conservation education, management and enforcement training programs.

• • •

EASY-TO-GET REFERENCES

"Outdoor Career Guide." Charles Manson, *Field and Stream*, April 1967. Contains essay on the variety of conservation openings and an excellent chart on job categories, education required, and salaries.

So You Want to be a Game Protector. Pennsylvania Game Commission, South Office Building, Harrisburg, Pa. 17105.

"Careers in Conservation" (reprint). *The Conservationist*, April-May, 1963, New York Department of Conservation, Albany, N. Y. 12226.

[10]

Specialty Jobs Closely Related to Conservation

The opportunities for service in fields closely related to conservation are as broad and unlimited as our total environment. The operation and management of wildlife, forests, fisheries and public health programs are a part of everyday life. So far, this presentation has catalogued the major classes of positions in these areas into several compartments. But there are others that cross lines and have an influence on the total effort. The story would not be complete without them.

SOME REPRESENTATIVE JOB DESCRIPTIONS

Conservation Education Specialist

Develops and implements conservation education programs within a state system by providing in-service training for field personnel engaged in conservation activities, school instructors and administrators; adapts course material to modern teaching methods and practices. Emphasizes the importance of environmental education within modern teaching methods and practices.

Education and Experience. College degree in resource management, journalism or closely related field. Two years professional experience.

Salary Range: $9,000—$12,000.

Excerpts from an actual state civil service job description for such a position in an Eastern state are as follows:

• • •

EXAMPLES OF WORK PERFORMED

Plans, develops, and implements wildlife conservation education programs.

Encourages and promotes fisheries or wildlife conservation education programs by conferring with education, conservation, civic agricultural, youth, and sportsmen's groups.

Supervises and participates in the preparation of motion pictures, slides, and other visual aids; prepares the story treatment and script for such visual aids; plans and participates in conservation education programs for radio and television presentation.

Plans, supervises, and maintains fisheries or wildlife conservation exhibits and cooperates with various museums in developing exhibit programs.

Plans, assigns, and directs subordinate personnel in conducting the fisheries or wildlife conservation education programs; prepares speech outlines and other materials for public presentation by field personnel.

Maintains close liaison with other state and Federal conservation agencies and with the State Department of Public Instruction to promote, develop, and conduct fisheries or wildlife conservation education courses.

Instructs field personnel, public school administrators, and instructors in conservation education programs and techniques.

Performs related work as required.

REQUIRED KNOWLEDGES, SKILLS, AND ABILITIES

Considerable knowledge of the principles and practices of game or fisheries conservation and management.

Considerable knowledge of the principles, practices, and techniques of fisheries or wildlife conservation education.

Knowledge of public relations techniques.

Knowledge of the available informational and educational materials related to the specialty practiced.

Some knowledge of the principles of effective supervision.

Ability to indicate the importance of conservation education to school administrators, public officials, and interested groups.

Ability to write and edit forms of informational and educational materials for films, course outlines, publications, and exhibits.

Ability to speak effectively before school administrators, instructors, and interested organizations.

Ability to train subordinate personnel and other educators in the techniques used to conduct conservation education programs as related to the specialty practiced.

Ability to express ideas clearly and concisely, orally and in writing.

Ability to establish and maintain effective working relationships with school administrators, state and Federal conservation personnel, other interested groups, and the public.

• • •

Photographic Specialist

Introductory technical position in field of photography, assisting superior in

taking and processing color and black and white pictures and slides for publicity, educational, informational, legal and record purposes.
Education and Experience: Graduation from high school.
Salary Range: $5,300—$7,000.

Chemistry Technician

Introductory technical work in chemistry, conducting standard tests to identify chemical compounds found in sewage, water, air, feeds and fertilizers.
Education and Experience: Associate degree including chemistry, technology and analysis or a related natural science.
Salary Range: $6,000—$8,000.

Chemist

Professional work in analysis and examination of chemical substances to determine elements and compounds; analyze water samples from industrial and mine drainages, sewage effluents and streams; tests dusts, fumes, vapors and other atmospheric substances to determine presence of toxic materials; testifies as witness in court as required.
Education and Experience: Bachelor's degree in chemistry.
Four years responsible experience.
Salary Range: $8,500—$11,000.

Botanist

Technician in field of botany conducts experiments and surveys on the introduction of noxious weeds, and methods of control of plants injurious to humans and animals. Must be familiar with plants and their characteristics.
Education and Experience: Master's college degree in agriculture.
Salary Range: $9,000—$12,000.

Experimental Biology Technician

Performs technical work in biological research in such areas as agriculture, forestry, fisheries, and wildlife, including observations, laboratory analysis and transposition of data into statistical form.
Education and Experience: College degree in biological science or appropriate field, or graduation from high school plus four years suitable experience.
Salary Range: $7,000—$9,000.

Roadside Development Engineer

Professional position in development and maintenance of roadside grounds and recreational areas. Controls erosion, plants nursery stock, seed and sod for highway beautification and conducts weed-control programs.
Education and Experience: College degree in landscape architecture, forestry, horticulture or agronomy. One year's experience in related work.
Salary Range: $8,000—$10,500.

Excerpts from an actual civil service job description for such a position in an Eastern state are as follows:

• • •

EXAMPLES OF WORK PERFORMED

Directs landscape and erosion control projects within a highway engineering district.

Makes preliminary field surveys; prepares complete plans, specifications, and estimates for planting or erosion control projects, and supervises its construction.

Inspects nursery stocks and sod for adherence to specifications with respect to disease, insects, virus, fungi, weeds, and root systems.

Inspects and approves seed, mulch, and similar materials used in roadside development projects.

Directs the control of noxious weeds and brush through herbicide spraying.

Inspects soils for chemical deficiencies and recommends remedial treatments.

Inspects lumber and posts as to species, quality, grade and suitability for the job which it is to be used.

Supervises the construction and maintenance of roadside rests.

Supervises issuance of permits for trimming existing trees and shrubs, plants and vines.

Performs related work as required.

REQUIRED KNOWLEDGES, SKILLS AND ABILITIES

Knowledge of those phases of landscape architecture, forestry, plant pathology, entomology, and horticulture, which apply to soil erosion control and the development and maintenance of roadside grounds and recreation areas.

Skill in directing proper sodding, seeding, and fertilizing methods and practices.

Ability to plan, develop and supervise planting and erosion control projects.

Ability to inspect nursery stock and supervise its planting and care.

Ability to supervise and direct the work of landscape aides and foremen.

• • •

Water Resources Analyst

Advanced technical assistance in development of state-wide water resource program, by analyzing water use project plans, both public and private, and making recommendations for appropriate action. This position correlates fish, game, forestry, recreation and similar programs with statewide water-use plans.

Education and Experience: College degree—major in wildlife, sport and commercial fisheries, hydraulic engineering or related science. Two years experience.

Salary Range: $12,500—$15,000.

Excerpts from an actual state civil service job description for such a position in a Western state are as follows:

• • •

EXAMPLES OF WORK

(Any one position may not include all of the duties listed nor do the listed examples include all tasks which may be found in positions of this class.)

Acts as the State Game or Fisheries Director's representative to the various intrastate and interagency water use groups; also negotiates with public and private agencies and organizations for the correction of existing situations where water use has eliminated runs of fish.

Acts as the State Game or Fisheries Director's representative in planning fish facilities at the proposed federally financed water projects.

Coordinates the stream improvement activities within the Game or Fish Commissions and with the numerous agencies of adjoining states and the Federal government, all of which engage in fish passage work.

Analyzes field and research data and recommend an appropriate decision to the Commission.

Reviews application to appropriate public water, and by delegated authority sends it to proper district supervisor for investigation.

Receives reports from district supervisor and prepares protest to the application when, from a fish and wildlife standpoint, the public interest is prejudiced.

Performs related work as required.

DESIRABLE KNOWLEDGES, SKILLS AND ABILITIES

Thorough knowledge of all phases of fisheries or game management.

Thorough knowledge of the problems confronting the Fish or Game Commissions in adopting water use projects to permit the survival of fish and game.

Thorough knowledge of the principles of plant and animal ecology.

Thorough knowledge of the state's fish resources including a knowledge of the habits and characteristics of salmon and other food and game fish procured from waters controlled by the state.

Working knowledge of hydraulics and the requirements for safe passage of salmonoid and other fish past obstructions.

Ability to establish and maintain effective working relationships with other governmental bodies, employers, other employees, with the commercial fish industry, sportsmen and with the general public.

Ability to speak effectively before others.

• • •

Ground Water Geologist

Professional position in the field of ground water geology, directing investigations in conjunction with state-wide water pollution control program and provides advisory services to State Sanitary Water Board on environmental problems.

Education and Experience: Ph.D. degree in geology. Three years professional experience.

Salary Range: $14,000—$19,000.

EASY-TO-GET REFERENCES

Landscape Architect. Two-page profile, U.S. Department of Agriculture, Forest Service, Washington, D.C. 20250.

"Careers in Conservation Education." (reprint) *The Conservationist.* Aug.-Sept., 1963, New York Department of Conservation, Albany, N.Y. 12226.

Careers in Botany. Botanical Society of America, Dept. of Botany, University of Texas, Austin, Texas 78710.

[11]

How to Get
These Kinds of Jobs

Conservation and protection of the environment is everyone's business
and the vast army of workers in the field are largely employed by public
agencies organized to perform the task.

In 1968, the distribution of employees in the natural resources field was approximately 216,000 Federal, 142,000 state and 35,000 local. An unknown number found employment with private industry, largely in the field of forestry.

WHERE TO START LOOKING

The best place to start looking for a job is in the local post office, Federal building, or state employment office. Announcements of forthcoming examinations are posted or are available through employment personnel. In some of the larger cities, Federal and state civil service offices combine for the convenience of job seekers.

Federal Service Entrance Examination announcements can be obtained through college placement offices and at other places where Federal employment information is distributed. State procedures vary, but college authorities or local state offices are happy to assist in guiding interested applicants to reliable sources of information. Examination announcements explain entrance requirements such as education and experience, and specify the entrance grade and salary range.

JOBS COVERED BY U.S. CIVIL SERVICE

Approximately 9 out of 10 jobs in the Federal Government in the United States are covered by the Civil Service Act, which the U.S. Civil Service Commission administers. This act was passed by the Congress to ensure that Federal employees are hired on the basis of individual merit and fitness. It provides for competitive examinations and the selection of new employees from among those who make the highest scores. The Commission, through its network of 65 Interagency Boards of Civil Service Examiners, is responsible for examining and rating applicants and supplying Federal departments and agencies with names of persons eligible for the jobs to be filled.

Civil service competitive examinations may be taken by all persons who are citizens of the United States, or who owe permanent allegiance to the United States (in the case of residents of American Samoa). To be eligible for appointment, an applicant must meet minimum age, training, and experience requirements for the particular position. A physical handicap will not in itself bar a person from a position if it does not interfere with his performance of the required duties. Examinations vary according to the types of positions for which they are held. Some examinations include written tests; others do not. Written examinations test the applicant's ability to do the job applied for or his ability to learn how to do it. In nonwritten examinations, applicants are rated on the basis of the experience and training described in their applications and any supporting evidence required.

Applicants are notified as to whether they have achieved eligible or ineligible ratings, and the names of eligible applicants are entered on a list in the order of their scores. When a Federal agency requests names of eligible applicants for a job vacancy, the interagency board sends the agency the names at the top of the appropriate list. The agency can select any one of the top three available eligibles. Names of those not selected are restored to the list for consideration for other job openings.

Appointments to civil service jobs are made without regard to an applicant's race, color, religion, national origin, politics, or sex.

U.S. WAGE BOARD EMPLOYEES

In addition to positions in the classified civil service, filled on the basis of competitive examinations, there is another large category known as "unclassified" or "wage board" employees.

Wage Board openings are filled by the individual agencies from their own registers, with guidelines and qualifications established to meet the agency needs. Rosters are made up of people who apply, listed by rank and order of application. Experience, education, and other pertinent data influence the ranking. Selections are then made from the roster.

Worker trainee appointments under this system are temporary, not to exceed 700 hours, beginning in June and ending in September. General civil service rules applying to selection by merit and prohibiting political activity are followed. Social Security is withheld. Sick and annual leave may be accumulated beginning after ninety days.

Worker trainee announcements for jobs in their area are issued by 56 civil service area offices, with at least one in each state.

Written tests are required to determine learning aptitude. Education and experience are considered. No written tests are required in some of the higher grades where experience and ability are paramount.

Wage Board rates are based on surveys in individual areas made by the Federal agencies and approved by the Civil Service Commission. They are comparable to rates paid by private industry.

STATE EMPLOYMENT

Personnel policies and hiring practices by the states vary rather widely. Some states, notably Michigan, Wisconsin, California, and New York have merit systems similar to the Federal Government. Others have programs where only technical and professional personnel are included. Some others, unfortunately, choose employees largely on the basis of the old "spoils" system.

The Book Of The States* lists numerous statistics and policies concerned with state governments. Under "Employment" are the following classes:

General

Thirty-eight states where most, but not all employees are covered by merit considerations.

Grant in Aid

Thirteen states cover employees on a merit basis if engaged in activities paid by Federal Grant-in-Aid funds. Another covers local employees only.

Other

Seven states select state police, health, welfare, and security personnel on a merit basis. There are a few combinations of General and Grant-in-Aid categories.

SOME TIPS ON JOB HUNTING

Regardless of where you are trying to get a job, there are some general principles to follow. Of these, the chief one to remember is that practically no job goes searching for an applicant—the job hunter must go to the position and the hiring source. Another one is that the job hunter must stay perpetually alert for a position opportunity, this suggesting that the more eyes and ears he has to supplement his own in search for possible vacancies, the better will be his chances.

Some other tips:

If a qualifying examination is required, try to get this done and out of the way as soon as possible. In many instances an applicant might not otherwise even secure serious consideration or an interview.

*Published by Council of State Governments, Iron Works Pike, Lexington, Kentucky 40505.

When there are listings of several or a number of qualified applicants for a position and your name is well down from the top of the list, do not become unduly discouraged. Some of those ahead of you may have secured other positions, moved away, etc., and no longer really be serious contenders for the position; this often improves your chances.

Your local state representative or assemblyman will likely be familiar with various opportunities; it might prove informative to check with him. For positions at the local level, your County Commissioner may have comparable information.

Occasionally, there are entry-level jobs which for various reasons seem to receive little attention from job seekers, yet a year's experience in such a position and earning a good recommendation usually sets up a winning combination for some better position later, whether in the same career field or elsewhere.

Finally, as opportunity arises to visit with someone holding the kind of position you would like to have, ask him how he got his job. This may not always elicit as much information as you would like to get, but in a good many cases you will at least get some helpful tips or useful clues.

[12]

Where to Write for Job Information

Information on the location and addresses of the various U. S. Civil
Service offices is so widely available that it is not included here. The interested reader should go to his nearest Post Office or Federal Office Building to
obtain details about where to apply and the necessary forms to use. The listings
which follow are therefore mainly of some of the lesser well-known agencies and
offices from which information regarding specialized fields of work and various
conservation programs and related career opportunities can be obtained.

REGIONAL OFFICES, BUREAU OF SPORT FISHERIES AND WILDLIFE

Pacific
   730 N. E. Pacific St., Portland, Oregon 97208

Southwest
   Federal Bldg., 500 Gold Ave., S. W., Albuquerque, N. M. 87103

North Central
   Federal Building, Ft. Snelling, Minneapolis, Minn. 55425

Southeast
   809 Peachtree, 7th Bldg., Seventh St. N. E., Atlanta, Georgia 30323

Northeast
   U. S. Post Office and Courthouse, Boston, Mass. 02109

REGIONAL OFFICES, NATIONAL PARK SERVICE

Northeast
143 South Third Street
Philadelphia, Pa. 19106

Southeast
Federal Building, Box 1008
400 North Eighth Street
Richmond, Va. 23240

Midwest
1709 Jackson Street
Omaha, Nebr. 68102

Southwest
Old Santa Fe Trail
P. O. Box 728
Santa Fe, N. Mex. 87501

Western
450 Golden Gate Avenue
P. O. Box 36063
San Francisco, Calif. 94102

National Capital
1100 Ohio Drive, S.W.
Washington, D. C. 20242

REGIONAL OFFICES, BUREAU OF OUTDOOR RECREATION

Northeast
Federal Bldg., 1421 Cherry St., Philadelphia, Pa. 19102

Southeast
810 New Walton Bldg., Atlanta, Georgia 30303

Lake Central
3853 Research Park Dr., Ann Arbor, Michigan 48104

Mid-Continent
Denver Federal Center, Denver, Colorado 80225

Pacific Northwest
U. S. Court House, Seattle, Washington 98104

Pacific Southwest
Box 36062, 450 Golden Gate Ave., San Francisco, California 94102

STATE DIRECTORS, BUREAU OF LAND MANAGEMENT

Alaska
555 Cordova Street
Anchorage, Alaska 99501

Arizona
Federal Building, Room 3022
Phoenix, Arizona 85025

California
Federal Office Bldg., Room E-2820
2800 Cottage Way
Sacramento, California 95825

Colorado
Federal Bldg., Room 14023
1961 Stout Street
Denver, Colorado 80202

Idaho
Federal Bldg., Room 334
550 West Fort Street
Boise, Idaho 83702

Montana
Federal Bldg. and U. S. Courthouse
316 N. 26th Street
Billings, Montana 59101

Nevada
Federal Bldg., 300 Booth St.,
Rm. 3008
Reno, Nevada 89502

New Mexico
U. S. Post Office and Federal Bldg.
South Federal Place, P. O. Box 1449
Santa Fe, New Mexico 87501

Washington-Oregon
729 N. E. Oregon St.,
P. O. Box 2965
Portland, Oregon 97208

Utah
Federal Bldg. 125 South State,
P. O. Box 11505
Salt Lake City, Utah 84111

Wyoming
U. S. Post Office and Courthouse Bldg.
2120 Capital Avenue, P. O. Box 1828
Cheyenne, Wyoming 82001

SERVICE CENTERS, BUREAU OF LAND MANAGEMENT

Denver
Building 53, Denver Federal Center
Denver, Colorado 80225

Portland
710 N. E. Holladay
P. O. Box 3861
Portland, Oregon 97208

REGIONAL OFFICES, FOREST SERVICE

Northern
Federal Bldg.,
Missoula, Mont. 59801

Rocky Mountain
Federal Center, Building 85,
Denver, Colo. 80225

Southwestern
517 Gold Avenue S.W.
Albuquerque, N. Mex. 87101

Intermountain
324 25th Street
Ogden, Utah 84401

California
630 Sansome Street
San Francisco, Calif. 84111

Pacific Northwest
319 SW Pine St., P. O. Box 3623
Portland, Oreg. 97208

Southern
50 Seventh St., N.E.
Atlanta, Ga. 30323

Eastern
633 West Wisconsin Ave.,
Milwaukee, Wis. 53203

Alaska
Federal Office Bldg. P. O. Box 1628
Juneau, Alaska 99801

REGIONAL OFFICES, SOIL CONSERVATION SERVICE

Northeast
Chester Pike,
Upper Darby, Pa. 19082

Southern
Federal Center,
Fort Worth, Tex. 76110

Midwest
134 S. 12th St.,
Lincoln, Neb. 68508

Western
507 Federal Bldg.,
701 N. W. Glisan St.,
Portland, Oregon, 97209

REGIONAL OFFICES, BUREAU OF COMMERCIAL FISHERIES

Pacific Northwest
  6116 Arcade Bldg.,
  Seattle, Washington 98101

Alaska
  P. O. Box 1668,
  Juneau, Alaska 99801

Gulf and South Atlantic
  144 First Ave. South
  St. Petersburg, Fla. 33701

Pacific Southwest
  101 Seaside Ave.,
  Terminal Island, Calif. 90731

North Atlantic Region
  Federal Bldg., 14 Elm St.,
  Gloucester, Mass. 01930

Great Lakes and Central
  5 Research Dr.,
  Ann Arbor, Mich. 48103

Hawaii
  2570 Dole St.,
  Honolulu, Hawaii 96812

REGIONAL OFFICES, FEDERAL WATER POLLUTION CONTROL ADMINISTRATION

Great Lakes
  33 E. Congress Pkwy,
  Chicago, Ill. 60605

Ohio Basin
  4676 Columbia Pkwy.,
  Cincinnati, Ohio 45226

Middle Atlantic
  918 Emmet St.,
  Charlottesville, Va. 22901

South Central
  1402 Elm St.,
  Dallas, Texas 75202

Missouri Basin
  911 Walnut St.,
  Kansas City, Mo. 64106

Southeast
  1421 Peachtree St.,
  Atlanta, Georgia 30309

Northeast
  Federal Bldg.
  Boston, Mass. 02203

Southwest
  760 Market St.,
  San Francisco, Cal. 74102

STATE POSITIONS

Departments of Conservation, Forestry, Fish and Game, Environment and Pollution Control, and others of similar nature are generally located at State Capitols. There are a few exceptions.

    In Kansas, the Forestry, Fish and Game Commission is located at Pratt.

    In Oregon, the Departments of Environmental Quality, Geology and Mineral Resources, Fish Commission, and Game Commission are located in Portland.

CONSERVATION DIRECTORY

The Conservation Directory, issued annually by the National Wildlife Federation, 1412 16th Street, N.W., Washington, D.C. 20036 is a valuable reference.

A typical recent edition contained 140 pages of conservation-oriented listings, including 57 U. S. Government agencies; 238 international, national, regional and interstate organizations and commissions; 310 government agencies and citizen groups in the United States and 50 in Canada.

Colleges and universities offering professional training in Natural Resource Management are listed in every state and in Nova Scotia, British Columbia, Ontario, Quebec, New Brunswick and Ontario, Canada.

STATE AND REGIONAL CONSERVATION COUNCILS

A directory listing clearing-house, shared-service and joint-action organizations formed by diverse environmental planning and conservation groups in states and regions of the United States is available through the Conservation Foundation, 1250 Connecticut Avenue, N.W., Washington, D. C. 20506.

NATIONAL PROFESSIONAL ORGANIZATIONS

American Fisheries Society
  Washington Bldg., 15th and New York Ave., N.W.,
  Washington, D.C. 20005

American Forestry Association
  919 17th St., N.W., Washington, D.C. 20006

Society of American Foresters
  1010 16th St., N.W., Washington, D.C. 20036

American Society of Range Management
  2120 S. Birch St., Denver, Colo. 80222

Ecological Society of America
  Connecticut College, New Haven, Conn. 06320

Izaak Walton League of America
  1326 Waukegan Rd., Glenview, Ill. 60025

National Wildlife Federation
  1412 16th St., N.W., Washington, D.C. 20036

Soil Conservation Society of America
  7515 N.E. Ankeny Rd., Ankeny, Iowa 50021

Sport Fishing Institute
  Suite 503, 719 13th St., N.W., Washington, D.C. 20005

Wildlife Management Institute
  709 Wire Bldg., Washington, D.C. 20005

Wildlife Society
  3900 Wisconsin Ave., Washington, D.C. 20016

EASY-TO-GET REFERENCES

Occupational Outlook Handbook. Bureau of Labor Statistics, U. S. Department of Labor, Washington, D.C. 20210.

Science and Engineering Careers in Government. Descriptions of beginning jobs, 21 pp. U. S. Government Printing Office, Washington, D.C. 20401. 30¢.

Career Opportunities in Oil and Gas. Special Report, Oil and Gas Journal, 211 S. Cheyenne St., Tulsa, Okla. 74101.

Occupational Brief No. 184 (geologists). Science Research Association, Inc., 259 Erie St., Chicago, Ill. 60611.

General Geological Professional Information. American Institute of Professional Geologists, P.O. Box 836, Golden, Colo. 80402.

[13]

Where to Get the Right Education

Within limited space it is not possible to present a complete listing of the universities and colleges offering natural-resource instruction in the many areas that comprise the total environmental field.

Because the opportunities for both undergraduate and graduate education are so varied, the individual should seek the kind of training that will best fit him for his chosen career. His own school authorities are the best starting point. Then, supplemental data may be secured from other sources.

The *Conservation Directory*, issued by the National Wildlife Federation, 1412 16th St., N.W., Washington, D.C. 20036, is an excellent source of information. It provides a list of colleges in all states and six in Canada, together with degrees granted in Forestry, Wildlife, Fisheries and Forest Recreation. This is the best condensed source of information on training possibilities in these professions.

A recent edition was available for $1.50.

Supplemental to this compilation, there follows a summary of colleges giving courses in range management and another covering soils and soil conservation.

Professional societies maintain current lists of institutions in the several disciplines and are happy to provide career guidance.

RANGE MANAGEMENT

University of Arizona
Department of
Watershed Management
Tucson, Arizona 85721

Brigham Young University
Department of Botany
Provo, Utah 84601

University of California
Department of Range Management
Berkeley, California 94820

Colorado State University
Department of Range Science
Fort Collins, Colorado 80521

Humboldt State College
Division of Natural Resources
Arcata, California 95521

University of Idaho
College of Forestry, Wildlife &
Range Sciences
Moscow, Idaho 83843

Kansas State University
Department of Agronomy
Manhattan, Kansas 66502

Fort Hays Kansas State College
Division of Biological Sciences
Fort Hays, Kansas 67602

University of Montana
School of Forestry
Missoula, Montana 59801

Montana State University
Department of Animal &
Range Sciences
Bozeman, Montana 50715

University of Nebraska
Department of Agronomy
Lincoln, Nebraska 68503

University of Nevada
Plant Science Department
Reno, Nevada 89507

New Mexico State University
Department of Animal,
Range & Wildlife Sciences
University Park, New Mexico 88001

North Dakota State University
Department of Botany
Fargo, North Dakota 58102

Oklahoma State University
Department of Agronomy
Stillwater, Oklahoma 74075

Oregon State University
Department of Range Management
Corvallis, Oregon 97331

South Dakota State University
Department of Animal Science
Brookings, South Dakota 57006

Sul Ross State College
Department of Animal Science
Alpine, Texas 79830

Texas A & M University
Department of Range Science
College Station, Texas 77843

Texas Technological College
Department of Agronomy &
Range Management
Lubbock, Texas 79409

Utah State University
Department of Range Science
Logan, Utah 84321

Washington State University
Department of Forestry &
Range Management
Pullman, Washington 99163

University of Wyoming
Plant Science Division
Laramie, Wyoming 82070

SOILS PLUS OTHER CONSERVATION SPECIALTIES

University of Arizona, Tucson, Arizona
Degree in Range Management and Watershed Management.
University of Arkansas, Fayetteville, Arkansas
   B. S. Degrees in Agriculture with majors in Agronomy, Soils; Agronomy, Crops and Agronomy, Range.
   B. S. Degrees in Agriculture and Civil Engineering.
California State Polytechnic College, San Luis Obispo, California
   Degree in Soil Science with emphasis on Soil Conservation.
Colorado State University, Fort Collins, Colorado
   Degree in Agronomy, with an option in Soil Conservation.
Delaware Valley College of Science and Agriculture, Doylestown, Pennsylvania
   Degree in Agronomy with emphasis on Soils and Soil and Water Conservation.
University of Florida, Gainesville, Florida
   Degree in Agriculture, with a major in Soils.
   Degree in Civil and Agriculture Engineering.
   Degree in Forest Management and Wildlife Management.
University of Georgia, Athens, Georgia
   Degree in Agriculture, with a "Concentration in Soil Conservation."
University of Hawaii, Honolulu, Hawaii
   Degree in Agriculture with major in Soil Science and on Tropical Soil Management and Fertility.
University of Idaho, Moscow, Idaho
   Degree in Agriculture Science with major in Field Crops and Soils.
   Degree in Forestry with major in Range Management, Wildlife Management and Forest Management.
   Degree in Engineering with major in Civil and Agriculture Engineering.
University of Illinois, Urbana, Illinois
   Degree in Agriculture, with emphasis on "Soil Conservation."
Purdue University, Lafayette, Indiana
   Degree in Agriculture, with a major in "Conservation Education."
Iowa State University, Ames, Iowa
   Degree in Forestry, with major in "Conservation, Range Management and Wildlife Management" on completion of 5th year of work.
   Degree in Agronomy with emphasis on Soil Conservation, Soil Survey and Land Appraisal.
   Degree in Agriculture Engineering with Soil and Water options.
Kansas State University, Manhattan, Kansas
   Degree in Agriculture, with a major in "Agronomy and Soil Conservation."
Fort Hays Kansas State College, Hays, Kansas
   Degree in Agriculture with major in Botany and Range Management.
University of Kentucky, Lexington, Kentucky
   Degree in Agriculture, with a major in "Agricultural Technology."
Louisiana State University, Baton Rouge, Louisiana
   Degree in Agricultural Engineering, with a "Soil Conservation Option."

Louisiana Polytechnic Institute, Ruston, Louisiana
  Degree in Forestry, with major in Soil Conservation.
University of Maine, Orono, Maine
  Degree in Agriculture with major in Agronomy and emphasis on Soil Conservation.
  Degree in Agriculture Engineering with emphasis on Soil and Water Conservation Engineering.
University of Massachusetts, Amherst, Massachusetts
  Degree in Agriculture, with major in Agronomy and specialization in Soil Conservation.
Michigan State University, East Lansing, Michigan
  Degree in Agriculture and Civil Engineering, Soil Science and Fisheries and Wildlife.
University of Minnesota, St. Paul, Minnesota
  Degree in Technical Agriculture, with major or minor in Soil Conservation.

Mississippi State University, State College, Mississippi
  Degree in Agronomy—Crops with courses in Soil Identification and Land Use and Soil Conservation.
  Degree in Agronomy—Soils with courses in Soil Fertility, Soil Identification and Land Use.
University of Missouri, Columbia, Missouri
  Degree in Agriculture, with a major in "Soil Conservation, Soil Survey and Land Appraisal." Degree in Agricultural Engineering, with major in "Soil and Water Control and Conservation."
Montana State University, Missoula, Montana
  Degree in Forest Conservation, with majors in Soil and Water Conservation and Watershed Management.
University of Nebraska, Lincoln, Nebraska
  Degree in Agriculture, with majors in Conservation, Range Management, and Technical Agronomy (Soils).
University of Nevada, Reno, Nevada
  Degree in Agriculture, with major in Range Management, Agronomy, and Soil Science.
New Mexico State University, State College, New Mexico
  Degree in Agriculture, with major in Range Management.
New York State College of Agriculture, Cornell University, Ithaca, New York
  Degree in Agriculture, with a major in Soil Conservation.
North Dakota State University, Fargo, North Dakota
  Degree in Agriculture with majors in Soil Fertility and Management.
  Degree in Agriculture Engineering with emphasis on Soil and Water Engineering. Degree in Soil Science with emphasis in Soil Conservation.
  Degree in Botany with emphasis in Range Management.
Ohio State University, Columbus, Ohio
  Degree in Agriculture, with major in Soil Conservation and opportunities for specializing in farm planning, soil conservation, wildlife management, general conservation, forestry, soil and water engineering and conservation education.

Ohio University, Athens, Ohio
Degree in Agriculture, with major in Soil Conservation.
Oklahoma Agricultural and Mechanical College, Stillwater, Oklahoma
Degree in Agricultural Engineering, with an option in Soil and Water control.
Degree in Agronomy with option in Soils, Field Crops and Range Management.
Oregon State University, Corvallis, Oregon
Degree in Agricultural Engineering with option in Soil and Water.
Degree in Agriculture with major in Range Management.
Pennsylvania State University, University Park, Pennsylvania
Degree in Agronomy with major in Soil Conservation.
A & M College of University of Puerto Rico
Degree in Agriculture with major in Plant Science.
University of Rhode Island, Kingston, Rhode Island
Degree in Agriculture with courses in Soil and Water Conservation.
South Dakota State College, Brookings, South Dakota
Degree in Agriculture with majors in Agronomy (Soils), Range Management and Wildlife Techniques with emphasis on Soil and Water Conservation.
Agricultural and Mechanical College of Texas, College Station, Texas
Degree in Agriculture Engineering with option in Soil and Water Conservation.
Degree in Agronomy with option in Soils and Crops. Degrees in Range and Forestry. Degrees in Plant and Soil Science.
Texas Technical College, Lubbock, Texas
Degree in Agriculture Engineering with option in Soil and Water Conservation.
Degree in Agronomy with options in Soils, Crops, and Range Management.
Abilene Christian College, Abilene, Texas
Degree in Agriculture with major in Range Management.
Southwest Texas State College, San Marcos, Texas
Degree in Agriculture with major in Range Management.
Sul Ross State College, Alpine, Texas
Degree in Agriculture with major in Range Management.
Utah State Agricultural College, Logan, Utah
Degree in Range Management, with a major in Soil Conservation and Watershed Management.

Virginia Polytechnic Institute, Blacksburg, Virginia
Degree in Forestry and Wildlife. Degree in Agronomy with Emphasis on Soil Management and Soil Classification. Degree in Agriculture Engineering with emphasis on Soil and Water Conservation.
Washington State University, Pullman, Washington
Degree in Conservation, with emphasis on conservation of Natural Resources.
University of Wisconsin, Madison, Wisconsin
Degree in Agriculture, with a conservation major in Agronomy or Soils, Farm Planning or Farm Management option.
Wisconsin State College, Platteville, Wisconsin
B. S. Degree in Agriculture with major in Soil Conservation.
Wisconsin State College, River Falls, Wisconsin
B. S. Degree in Agriculture with major in Soil Conservation.

University of Wyoming, Laramie, Wyoming
Degree in Agriculture, with majors in Range Management, and Soils.
Degree in Agriculture Engineering with option in Soil and Water.

CORRESPONDENCE SCHOOLS

Generally, correspondence courses do not count toward basic education required for aides or technical jobs with public agencies. They may be counted as "bonus points," however, in qualifying for a job. They can broaden the student's knowledge of conservation programs and be a distinct asset in passing Civil Service tests. Correspondence courses are helpful, too, for a job holder interested in self-improvement leading to promotions and better pay.

Home study courses are becoming increasingly important in the education field. The U. S. Office of Education states: "Each year, more people enroll in accredited private home-study schools than enter all colleges as freshmen."

The National Home Study Council, of Washington, D.C. maintains an Accrediting Commission listed by the U.S. Office of Education as a "nationally recognized accrediting agency." The Council is almost fifty years old, and its latest brochure lists 137 accredited home-study schools which meet high standards of faculty, up-to-date courses, and educational service, ample student success, reasonable tuition charges, truthful advertising, and sound financial ability.

The Council lists two accredited schools in the field of Conservation:

1. NATIONAL SCHOOL OF CONSERVATION, 1129 20th St., N. W., Washington, D.C. 20036. Founded 1958. Provides a 5-part course in conservation of natural resources: (1) Foundation of Natural Resources. (2) Fish and Wildlife Conservation, (3) General Forestry, (4) Soil, Water and Range Conservation, (5) Parks and Outdoor Recreation. General and technical instruction prepares men and women for Civil Service examinations of state and Federal conservation agencies, as well as for employment in private conservation organizations. Aids citizen leadership and assists landowners in the management of their properties. Maintains a field training facility at Wolf Springs Forest, Minong, Wisconsin.

Details concerning the 5-part course were supplied by the National School of Conservation as quoted below:

FOUNDATION COURSE

Lesson 1. The Field of Conservation. Training for a career, job opportunities, conservation programs, types of duties in Forestry, Wildlife, Soil and Range Conservation, Park Rangers, Outdoormanship.

Lesson 2. Our Basic Natural Resources. History of the conservation movement.

Lesson 3. Ecology—Nature's Communities. Basic Soil Characteristics, Moisture, Slope, Air Movement, Climate, Plant Communities, Succession, Nature's Pyramid, Plant and Animal Associations, Balance of Nature.

Lesson 4. Nature and Man. Quality in our environment—air, water and the land, causes of deterioration.

Lesson 5. Protecting Our Natural Resources. Forest Fires—Behavior, Prevention, Equipment.

Lesson 6. Conservation Organizations and Their Jobs. Federal Government —State Departments of Conservation.

FISH & WILDLIFE CONSERVATION

Lesson 7. Principles of Wildlife Biology. Observing wildlife; Populations; The animal community. Glossary of wildlife terms.

Lesson 8. Wildlife Management Techniques. Wildlife management plan; Steps to sound management; Habitat management.

Lesson 9. Fisheries Biology and Management. Ecology of fishing waters— basic requirements; Classes of fish species; Management measures.

Lesson 10. Conservation Law Enforcement. Hunting and fishing regulations; Law enforcement; Predator control.

GENERAL FORESTRY

Lesson 11. Surveying and Mapping Land Areas. Systems of land subdivision; Making a map; Topographic maps; Drafting.

Lesson 12. Identification Silvics; Tree Species by Characteristics.

Lesson 13. Forest Management and Silviculture. Reforestation, Species Choice, Intermediate Cuttings; Sustained Yield Rotations and Cutting Cycles.

Lesson 14. Measuring and Managing the Forest. Mapping the Forest Cover Types; Growth Management.

Lesson 15. Harvesting, Processing, and Marketing. Logging Methods by Forest Types, Sealing Sawlogs and Pulpwood; Processing Lumber and Veneer, Pulp and Paper.

Lesson 16. Multiple Uses of The Forest. Forest landscapes, Watershed Conservation Measures, Forest Recreation.

SOIL, WATER & RANGE CONSERVATION

Lesson 17. Soil Conservation on Agricultural Lands. Soils—Characteristics and Quality; Soil Conservation Measures; Wind Erosion; Irrigation and Drainage.

Lesson 18. Special Soil Conservation Practices. Stabilizing Streambanks; Roadbank Stabilization; Recreation Lands; Metropolitan Areas.

Lesson 19. Conservation of The Western Range. Livestock and the Grassland Resource; Range Surveys and Condition; Ranch Conservation Plans; Range Conservation Practices—Renovation of pastures; Managing Forest Lands for Grazing.

Lesson 20. Conservation of Water and Watersheds. Water Resources—Hydrologic Cycle, Streamflow and Runoff—Forest Watershed Management; Water Pollution Control.

PARKS AND OUTDOOR RECREATION

Lesson 21. Outdoor Recreation Areas and Activities. Americans and Their Outdoor Recreation, National and State Parks and Forests, County and Municipal Parks, Wilderness Areas.

Lesson 22. Planning Recreational Area Uses. Recreation Management Plans.
Lesson 23. Design and Construction of Recreational Improvements. Structures and Facilities—Nature Trails, Overlooks, Visitor Centers and Interpretation.
Lesson 24. Management of Recreational Uses. Directing Visitor Flow, Park and Nature Interpretation, Safety Measures, Law Enforcement, Water Sports Management.
Lesson 25. Administration of Park and Recreational Lands. Organization of Administrative Functions.

2. NORTH AMERICAN SCHOOL OF CONSERVATION, 4401 Birch Street, Newport Beach, California 92660. Founded 1959. Courses offered to prepare for vocational careers with Federal, state and private organizations. Their 100-lesson course covers all phases of conservation including instruction in wildlife management, fish management, forest management, park management and soil and range management. A division of North American Correspondence Schools—National Systems Corporation.

This school summarizes their course as follows:

SECTIONS I & II. GAME MANAGEMENT

Careers in Game Management
History of Game Conservation
Big Game Management
Small Game Management
Fur-bearing Animal Management
Game Bird Management
Waterfowl Management

Refuge Management
Predators and Predator Control
Migration
Game Laws
Law Enforcement
Your Role in Game Management

SECTIONS III & IV. FISH MANAGEMENT

Careers in Fish Management
History of Fish Conservation
Game Fish Management
Cold Water Fish Management
Warm Water Fish Management
Trout Management

Hatchery Management
Stocking, Spawning,
Sampling & Tagging
Population Control
Pollution Detection
Your Role in Fish Management

SECTIONS V & VI. FORESTRY MANAGEMENT

Careers in Forestry Management
History of Forestry Conservation
The Government's Role in Forestry
Anatomy of a Tree
Forest Management
Planting, Thinning and Pruning
Forest Fire Prevention

Insect Control
Disease Control
Timber Management
Park Management
Our National Parks
Your Role in Forestry Management

SECTIONS VII & VIII. SOIL MANAGEMENT

Careers in Soil Management
History of Soil Conservation
Planning for the Farm

Land Use
Crop Rotation and Plant Management
Contour Farming

MAKING A LIVING IN CONSERVATION

Strip Cropping
Terracing
Grasslands, Rangelands and Woodlands
Moisture, Irrigation and Waterways

Farm Pools & Drainage
Nutrients & Fertilizers
Erosion
Your Role in Soil Management

SECTIONS IX & X. JOB OPPORTUNITIES

Careers in Conservation
Your Life as a Conservationist
Conservation Pay Scales
How to Pick a Job and Land It
How to Apply for a Job
How to Handle the Interview
How to Study
Civil Service Exams and How to Prepare

for Them
Government Conservation Organizations
Federal Positions
State Positions
Positions in Private Industry
Self-Employment Opportunities
How to Succeed in Conservation
Your Role in Conservation

EASY-TO-GET-REFERENCES

Conservation Directory. Published annually by the National Wildlife Federation, 1412 16th St., N.W., Washington, D. C. 20036. Contains list of international, federal, regional, and state conservation agencies and organizations and officials and a list of colleges offering conservation training. $1.50.

Careers in Mineral Industries. The Pennsylvania State University, College of Mineral Industries, University Park, Pa. 97203.

Preparing for a Career in Range Management. American Society of Range Management, 2120 S. Birch St., Denver, Colo. 80222.

Career Opportunities in Rangeland Management. American Society of Range Management, 2120 S. Birch St., Denver, Colo. 80222.

Fisheries Science and Related Courses in North American Colleges and Universities. Sport Fishing Institute, Suite 503, 719 13th St., N.W., Washington, D. C. 20005. (Free only to career guidance officers; $1.00 otherwise.)

Forestry Schools in the United States. FS-9, U. S. Government Printing Office, Washington, D. C. 20210. 15¢.

Universities and Colleges with Wildlife Management and Conservation Curricula in North America. The Wildlife Society, 1900 Penna. Ave., Washington, D. C. 20006.

Careers for Women in Forestry—Wildlife Management Option. West Virginia University, Morgantown, W. Va. 26506.

Colleges and Universities that offer Environmental, Conservation Education Programs. Department of Health, Education and Welfare, Office of Education, Washington, D. C. 20202.